Dirt and Stardust

Dirt and Stardust

Finding Jesus in the Sermon on the Mount

JEREMY DUNCAN

Foreword by Bobbi Salkeld

RESOURCE *Publications* • Eugene, Oregon

DIRT AND STARDUST
Finding Jesus in the Sermon on the Mount

Resource Publications
An Imprint of Wipf and Stock Publishers
199 W. 8th Ave., Suite 3
Eugene, OR 97401

www.wipfandstock.com

PAPERBACK ISBN: 978-1-6667-3271-9
HARDCOVER ISBN: 978-1-6667-2671-8
EBOOK ISBN: 978-1-6667-2672-5

.   NOVEMBER 2, 2021 2:51 PM

*To the community at Commons, who allow me
to think and write and speak and learn along with you.*

Contents

Foreword by Bobbi Salkeld | *ix*

INTRODUCTION
  Who Am I to You? | *1*

CHAPTER ONE
  Making Sense Is Missing the Point | *7*

CHAPTER TWO
  Salt and Light | *22*

CHAPTER THREE
  Turning the Law on Its Head | *32*

CHAPTER FOUR
  You Have Heard It Said | *44*

CHAPTER FIVE
  The Intent of Righteousness | *59*

CHAPTER SIX

Aligning Ourselves with God | *66*

CHAPTER SEVEN

Resting in God's Goodness | *80*

CHAPTER EIGHT

God's Idea of the Good Life | *88*

CHAPTER NINE

Judging As God Judges | *96*

CHAPTER TEN

Asking, Seeking, and Knocking | *106*

CHAPTER ELEVEN

The Hidden Path | *115*

CONCLUSION

The Power of Resiliency | *125*

About the Author | *127*

Endnotes | *129*

Bibliography | *135*

Foreword

IN 2016, I LEFT MY LIFE in Vancouver, British Columbia, to make a new life in Calgary, Alberta. Leaving behind my friends, my professional networks, and one of Canada's prettiest cities to start over again was a change that didn't make perfect sense. But after seeking and finding love in my life, I felt ready for new growth.

One uneasy feeling persisted, however, as I drove through the mountains, newly married. For fifteen years, I had loved the work of being a pastor. I loved preaching. I loved leading. I loved caring. As we drove on winter roads, I wondered, "When I get to this new city, who will have me? Where will I work?" I had no leads, no ideas about churches in Calgary, and no sense that I would fit in.

But soon after arriving, a couple of good friends suggested I try Commons. I didn't know the church, but my friends had faith while I worried. As I searched for an email address, I thought, "What do I have to lose?" I sent a message to introduce myself. The reply came quickly: "Come by for a coffee. Let's talk." And that's when I met Jeremy Duncan.

Jeremy's openness to something new is central in leading Commons. He had no idea I was about to come knocking on the door for a job, but he opened it, made a couple of great cappuccinos, and basically, we got right to work. We talked theology, the story of Commons, and the teaching of Jesus. I don't remember us talking about the Sermon on the Mount specifically, but the themes were there: justice, prayer, interpretation.

One of the best things about Jesus' teaching in the Sermon on the Mount is that it doesn't always make sense. Of course, some sections are easy to understand. *Blessed are the merciful, for they will be shown mercy. Take reconciliation as seriously as you take your worship. Build your house—your very life—on a stable foundation.* But then, there are sections in the Sermon where meaning is harder to decipher. *Who exactly are the poor in spirit? What's Jesus' relationship to the law? What does Jesus mean by "righteousness"?*

You can live in this balance between clarity and fog for a long time, until you can't. Eventually, the questions you have about who Jesus is and what Jesus says will become an unbalance you cannot ignore. This predicament is part of a relationship with faith—where you either reach for more or let the whole thing go.

I've teetered on faith's edge, and I'm sure you have too. You've had trouble making sense of scripture. You've felt hurt by unanswered prayer. You've lived with long seasons of uncertainty. But eventually, some new study, some new wisdom, some new ideas find you and inspire you to keep going. Your faith grows, and you grow.

Dirt and Stardust allows you to keep growing. You will find new ways to think about righteousness, more profound ways to think about generosity, and hospitable ways to think about Christian presence in the world. Jeremy will amplify the Lord's Prayer, expand a concept of eternity, and increase your fascination with forgiveness. The parts of Jesus' teaching you love will be more endearing to you, while the details that make you wrinkle up your nose or close your Bible app in confusion will make more sense in their context.

The Sermon on the Mount offers an excellent thought experiment: If all you know about God is in these three chapters, who will you be? Matthew chapters 5–7 teach that God cares for those who struggle and offers them that care through you. You aren't waiting for God to be salt and light; you are salt and light. You don't need to make a big deal out of one act of generosity; you get to be discreetly generous all the time. You haven't had to earn God's love; you're living right in the middle of it.

Working at Commons with Jeremy, our team, and a community captivated by Jesus changed my life. On that drive through the mountains to Calgary, I couldn't sense how God was inviting me to grow through my worry. But this growth has been the best growth of my life. I've grown as a pastor. I've grown as a friend. I've grown with God—who always offers me more good than I can imagine for myself.

Goodness is under our feet and above our heads—dirt and stardust, all places to reencounter the Divine. Read this book. Learn from this book. And then, keep growing.

Bobbi Salkeld
Eastertide 2021

INTRODUCTION

WHO AM I TO YOU?

The Sermon on the Mount is the single most important biblical text in the history of Christian ethics and for understanding how we should live. It is the longest single block of Jesus' teaching that we have in the Synoptic Gospels. [1]

—DAVID GUSHEE

IN HER BOOK ON Jesus' parables, Amy-Jill Levine opens with a note of thankfulness for the fact that the majority of Jesus' interpretations did not make their way to us. She writes, "the Gospel writers, in their wisdom, left most of the parables as open narratives in order to invite us into engagement with them."[2] While she is focused on Jesus' parables in her book, Levine has highlighted one of the critical elements that continue to make Jesus a compelling figure today. The fact that his teaching intentionally invites our participation with him. Rather than giving us easy answers, Jesus forces us to think about what he is saying. He welcomes our frustrations both with him and the material, and I really like that about him.

However, Levine also makes a provocative observation about Jesus' closest friends, and by extension us. She says the disciples "were looking for something within their comfort zone and, like many, resisted what the parables might convey."[3] This observation, I think, is vital for anyone who comes to Jesus' teaching. It is precisely because Jesus leaves room for us to enter into the process of learning, that if we're not careful, we can very easily massage Jesus' words to fit neatly into our expectations. Jesus leaves room for us to interpret, but he also leaves room for us to miss the point; to turn him into yet another religious guru selling Divine love on the other side of religious obligation.

SPACE FOR US

This book is about finding Jesus in the Sermon on the Mount, but there's a story a little later in Matthew that might be useful for us by way of introduction to Jesus. Truthfully, the same story shows up in Matthew, Mark and Luke, which is a solid indication that it was treasured within the early Christian communities. A lot of these Jesus tales were being passed around, after all, but this one everyone knew.

Jesus has just fed 4000 people with seven loaves of bread and a few small fish to set the stage. This miracle is one of his favorites, and you might remember it from other moments like two chapters earlier where Jesus fed 5000 people with fives loaves and two fish. Setting aside the practicalities of how something like this happens, addressing hunger is a focus for Jesus and that in itself is worth paying attention to. Jesus doesn't divide the human experience into physical and spiritual; he embraces what it means to be human as an integrated whole.

Later that day is where things get interesting though. After being confronted by some critics he uses the experience as a teaching moment for his disciples.

Jesus came to the region of Caesarea Philippi, he asked his disciples, "Who do people say the Son of Man is?" They replied, "Some say John the Baptist; others say Elijah; and still others, Jeremiah or one of the prophets." "But what about you?" he asked. "Who do you say I am?
— *Matthew 16:13–15*

I can feel for Jesus here. No one wants to be mistaken for someone else. I suppose if you are mistaken for a celebrity that might ease the sting though, and that's along the lines of what happens here. The disciples respond to his question telling him that some of the people think he is John the Baptist, back from the dead. John had sadly been executed earlier (Matthew 14:11–12). Others are saying that Jesus is Elijah returned, which is also kind of a big deal, since, in the Hebrew Scriptures, Elijah was taken up into heaven by a chariot of fire (2 Kings 2:11). Still, others are suggesting Jeremiah or one of the prophets as Jesus' true identity. This one is perhaps not as dramatic as the first two options, but certainly a confirmation that Jesus is a becoming a big deal in the eyes of the public. Remember, this conversation is happening directly on the heels of Jesus feeding 4000 people with a few scraps of food, so these kinds of celebrity comparisons make sense.

Jesus of course, wants to hear what his disciples think of him. That's where the conversation is heading, after all. At the same time though, I don't think this opening inquiry is just here to fill time. Jesus has been teaching and healing and feeding people for a while now. His reputation has been growing in this region of the Roman Empire. He probably is intrigued to hear what the crowds are saying about him. I know I would be. And yet, what he hears from his friends is that people are still confused about who he really is. I imagine there is something lonely in that. For me, this moment with Jesus asking his friends if the crowds really "get him" has got to be one of the most relatable images in the Gospels.

He continues though.

"And you?" He asks, "Who do you say I am?"

I find myself intrigued by this moment.

Jesus starts by asking an arms-length question about what the crowds are saying. He even distances himself from the question a bit by asking about the "Son of Man." But now he pulls the conversation in tighter and makes it more personal. "And you? What do you say about me?"

There's a shift here from the title, "Son of Man" to the first person. There's also the repetition of the second person pronoun. "And you, what do you say about me?" It all just feels more intimate than the first question, doesn't it? I think that's intentional. I think Jesus is doing this on purpose. After all we do this in our conversations too, this easing our way toward what we really want to ask.

I have coffee with people from my church community all the time, and most people that ask for a coffee with me have something they want to get to—eventually. It's the rare person, who sits down, takes a sip of their latte, and says precisely what's on their mind. We tend to work our way up to those things once we feel safe.

Here, in a quiet moment, away from the crowds, after being confronted by critics, when finally, no one is watching or waiting to catch him, Jesus turns to his friends for reassurance. He starts at the edge of the conversation. "What are people saying about me? Are they paying attention to me? Do you think they get it?" But then when his friends respond and let him know that yes, the crowds are paying attention, but no, they don't quite understand, it's now that Jesus asks what he has wanted to. "And you? what about you? Do you get it? Do you see what's happening here? Do you know who I really am?"

In one sense, this is a profound theological moment. Peter is about to declare Jesus the Messiah for the very first time. At another level though, maybe even a more significant level, this is a profoundly personal moment for these two friends.

Imagine after all this time, after all these parables and miracles and teaching, imagine Peter had said to Jesus, "to be honest, we're not sure what to make of you either." It can be vulnerable to see ourselves through someone else's eyes. Maybe it was for Jesus too.

But then, on the other side, there's Peter. He responds, "You are the Messiah, the Son of the living God" (Matthew 16:16) and that's the right answer for sure. But think about this moment from his perspective. Peter's been with Jesus for a while now. He's been following him around, listening to him teach. He's seen things he can't explain—up close. He even left his home, his job, and his family to follow Jesus. Whatever you imagine about Peter and all his failings, Peter is a Jesus follower.

But that makes me think that this can't be the moment where Peter decided that Jesus was the Messiah. I don't know when that happened exactly—maybe it was the first moment Peter left his fishing nets to follow Jesus—who can say? This however, I'm convinced, was not that moment. It was the first time he had said it out loud though. And that's significant.

Sometimes we realize a thing, and we carry that thing around with us for a very long time before we ever allow ourselves to say it out loud. Sometimes the more important that thing is, the more life-shaping it is, the longer we hold onto it silently waiting for just the right moment to give it voice.

I can imagine Peter holding these words in his mouth, biting his tongue around fires and over meals. I imagine him walking down dusty roads and sitting in crowds listening to Jesus unfold the kingdom of God and desperately wanting to say it. I bet Peter had these words on the tip of his tongue a hundred times before but never found the courage to put any breath behind them. Because, what if he did?

What if Peter had put all this time, and all this effort in, left everything behind, and what if Jesus wasn't who he thought he was? It can be a scary moment to say out loud the thing you hope for most in the world. Maybe that's the point of the story.

The Divine Word of God steps into human history, makes friends, and then makes space for his friends to name what's happening. Everything Peter hopes for, everything he has come to believe, everything he trusts in the world is standing right in front of him and Jesus makes space for him to be the one to name it.

This is part of what I love about Jesus because I'm convinced that space, in that moment, was not a test to pass or fail. It was an invitation for Peter to say what he hoped for more than anything. My trust is that Jesus still makes that space for us today—to come to his words not as exam but as an invitation to encounter our deepest hopes for God.

This book started as a series of sermons—an attempt to preach my way through the Sermon on the Mount—but as I wrote and spoke and fell into the inevitable conversations that followed, I found myself slowly reminded of this profound invitation. Not simply to accept Jesus as savior but to allow Jesus to shape what I hope for most in the world—to believe that everything from the dirt beneath my feet to the stars that fill the night sky are bound up in his way. I trust that one day, I might even get the chance to say it out loud to him.

CHAPTER ONE

MAKING SENSE IS MISSING THE POINT

THE SERMON ON THE Mount was Jesus' first major public address, so engaging with it is sort of like jumping in with ground-floor, day-one, early-adopter, knew-him-before-he-was-famous Jesus. In this chapter, we're going to move through the first ten verses, traditionally known as the Beatitudes. But we will focus mainly on the first three, because really, they set the stage for everything else that follows in Jesus' sermon and in this book.

FROM ALL WALKS OF LIFE

In the Sermon on the Mount, we hear from a fresh-faced Jesus who has just launched his public ministry. He's been moving through the region, teaching and healing and performing some miracles. The buzz has been building, and a crowd gathers to hear him, so Jesus pauses to address them. The sermon runs from Matthew chapter 5 to the end of chapter 7. But let's back up, to the end of chapter 4, to set the stage:

> *Jesus went throughout Galilee, teaching in their syna-*
> *gogues, proclaiming the good news of the kingdom, and*

healing every disease and sickness among the people. News about him spread all over Syria [obviously], and people brought to him all who were ill with various diseases, those suffering severe pain, the demon-possessed, those having seizures, and the paralyzed; and he healed them. Large crowds from Galilee, the Decapolis, Jerusalem, Judea and the region across the Jordan followed him.

Now when Jesus saw the crowds, he went up on a mountainside and sat down. His disciples came to him, and he began to teach them.

—*Matthew 4:23–5:2*

So here's what we have to picture in our minds: a huge crowd of people, come from all over to hear Jesus. Noticing the crowd, Jesus climbs a hill so they can see him. His closest friends draw close to him, and he teaches them in this sort of public, open-air address.

To really grasp what he's saying, though, we have to notice the people Jesus is talking to, here. It says, "Large crowds from Galilee, the Decapolis, Jerusalem, Judea and the region across the Jordan." Now, Galilee is where Jesus is from. This is a very Jewish, religious, blue-collar region, so to speak. These are Jesus' people—not from the cultural centre of Jerusalem, but from the biblical equivalent of flyover country. The specific people in the audience may be strangers to him, but he knows them; he grew up with them. Jesus *gets* these people.

Then there is the more cosmopolitan part of the crowd, the people from Jerusalem, including the religious leaders within Jewish culture. They likely have a higher-level grasp of power, politics, and the machinations of Rome. Although they are religious like the Galileans, their sense of sophistication differentiates them from the rural sort of folks Jesus knows from his childhood. When word about Jesus was just beginning to spread, a man Nathaniel was asked if he'd heard of him, and Nathaniel replied, "Can anything good come from Nazareth?" That's the kind of attitude you might expect from Jerusalem.

But we've also got the Decapolis tucked in here. *Decapolis* meant "Ten Cities," a collection of Greco-Roman cities southeast of Galilee. These were not Jewish people, and in the eyes of a Jewish person, at least, these were not religious people, either. In fact, for a lot of the people Jesus has grown up with, and certainly for the religious leaders from the city, these people from Decapolis are to be avoided assiduously.

So here they are, mashed together: blue-collar Jews, big-city moguls, and Greek and Roman pagans. All sorts of people, from all walks of life, have come to see what this guy from Nazareth has to say.

THE MEANING OF "MEEK"

The word *beatitude*[4] is derived from the Latin translation of the word *makarios*[5], which is the Greek word translated as "blessed" in Matthew 5. These are a series of eight declarations known as the Beatitudes, which is how Jesus starts his address.

> *He began to teach them.*
> *He said: "Blessed are the poor in spirit, for theirs is the kingdom of heaven. Blessed are those who mourn, for they will be comforted. Blessed are the meek, for they will inherit the earth. Blessed are those who hunger and thirst for righteousness, for they will be filled. Blessed are the merciful, for they will be shown mercy. Blessed are the pure in heart, for they will see God. Blessed are the peacemakers, for they will be called children of God. Blessed are those who are persecuted because of righteousness, for theirs is the kingdom of heaven."*
> —*Matthew 5:2–10*

Have you ever read these statements and thought to yourself, at least for a second, "What on earth is going on here? This sounds nice, but none of it makes any sense. This isn't how the real world works!" Is Jesus just trolling us here?

Instead of trying to absorb what Jesus is saying—instead of trying to allow his imagination to infect ours—we instead work on trying to fit his words, his dream, into our world. We try to make it make sense, and I don't think that works. Because the truth is, I don't think Jesus is trying to make sense of our world; he's trying to upend our sense of the world.

Take this one: "Blessed are the meek, for they will inherit the earth." I've been told that meekness means strength under control. This means that the meek are in fact powerful, but they know how and when to use their power, which is why they'll inherent the earth when the time is right.

Except that's clearly not what *meek* means, at least not in English. *Meek* means "submissive" or "easily imposed upon." The Greek word here is *praus*, but that doesn't mean strength under control, either—it means "not being overly impressed by a sense of one's self-importance, *gentle, humble, considerate, meek*." [6] And in fact, the Hebrew equivalent is the word 'anah, which means "to crouch or bow." [7] So there is nothing in this word *meek*, whether you are reading it in English, Greek, or Hebrew, that should give you the image of coiled strength just waiting to be let loose. The only reason to read it that way is to make Jesus make sense in the world with which we're familiar.

But what if Jesus isn't trying to be familiar here? What if he's trying to be disruptive? What if Jesus is actually saying what he seems to be saying—that the easily overpowered, not overly impressive, bowed down, and cowering *will* inherit the earth?

You see, we tend to read this through our modern Western assumptions and try to imagine Jesus saying something like it in our world. And when that doesn't work, we often substitute our common sense for Jesus' decidedly uncommon perspective. However, if you're a Jewish person—particularly a poor Jewish person—standing in the audience, you know what's he's saying here. It probably brings to mind Psalm 37, which is all about the wicked using their wealth and power to grind down the righteous, who will still eventually "inherit the land" (v. 11) because God will "[help] them and deliver them" (v. 40).

The meek are not the powerful under control. The meek are not the strong waiting for the right moment to spring. The meek are those who have been crushed and oppressed. The meek include those have had their land taken from them by the more powerful.

The meek are those who know they don't have the power to fight back. So, instead of counting on their power, they hope for a new world—a more just world—to come to them. In the Jewish culture, it was called "the world to come."[8]

You can imagine that if a Greek or Roman person from the Decapolis, a descendant of colonists (to use a modern term), is standing beside a Jewish person indigenous to Jerusalem, listening to Jesus from Galilee talk about the return of land, this is an awkward moment. Even though it often looks like the people who have the courage, strength, power, and ambition to "get theirs" are carving up the world and distributing it among themselves, Jesus says it doesn't have to be like that.

Jesus isn't trying to explain why the meek *deserve* the world. Nothing in the word *meek* corresponds to any quality that deserves an inheritance according to our assumed standards. No, this is Jesus saying that maybe our imagination of who deserves what is the problem to begin with. And against expectation, he implies, it's not the type of people who always seem to be on top of the world and running the show that always will remain on top.

You see, this Sermon on the Mount has some brilliant advice for us, but first and foremost, it is a declaration of what Jesus imagines waiting for us, just below the surface of what we're used to seeing in the world. Once you get a glimpse of that—as soon as you get what Jesus is doing here, that he's not explaining our world to us but declaring a new world among us—then all of these beatitudes, these eight declarations of how the world could be, stop needing to be so sensible. They become aspirational instead. Jesus isn't explaining the world as it is; he's describing the world as it could be.

POVERTY OF SPIRIT

But let's return to the starting point, now. Jesus says, "Blessed are the poor in spirit, for theirs is the kingdom of heaven." In my opinion, this is possibly the most important statement in the entire corpus of Jesus' words. If we miss this, I think we risk missing everything that follows.

Just like with meekness, if we try to turn this beatitude into our goal, we miss the point. Poverty of spirit is not something to aspire to. Poverty of spirit is not something admirable. It does not mean humility, or even an awareness of your need for God. Simply put, it means spiritual insufficiency.

Jesus is not attempting to run counter-programming to his likely original form[9] of the beatitude found in Luke 6:20, "Blessed are you who are poor, for yours is the kingdom of God"; he is expanding the same idea here for a new audience. Just as the poor lack the financial resources they need, so also the spiritually poor lack the religious resources they need. This is about complete and utter confusion when it comes to the things of God—the inability to comprehend God. In other words, "Blessed are you who have no clue." Philosopher Dallas Willard writes, "Blessed are the spiritual zeros—the spiritually bankrupt, deprived and deficient, the spiritual beggars, those without a wisp of 'religion'—when the kingdom of the heavens comes upon them."[10] That's who is blessed, because that is the Good News.

When you've had your slice of the pie taken from you, when you've had suffering inflicted on you, when you have nowhere else to go and no plan for where to turn, or when all of your choices only seem to make everything worse and everyone knows it, the good news is that God is still *for* you—and always has been.

We really do tend to struggle with this, because it doesn't make sense to us, so we keep searching for something meritorious in each blessing: "Well, the meek are self-controlled, and those who mourn are in touch with their emotions, and the poor in spirit are at least honest about their need for God." But that's not what Jesus is saying here. Jesus is saying our concept of the Divine and who deserves God's attention is fundamentally upside down. And that's why, before Jesus can tell us anything about ourselves, he needs to tell us about God.

GOD IS FOR YOU

Now, we've already talked about the audience. So, if you're listening to Jesus' sermon, maybe you're a Roman pagan or a Galilean day-laborer. Maybe you're a religious leader from Jerusalem. Regardless, let's get this straight from the start: *God is for you.* Though, let me clarify: God is for you, and God is also for the person beside you. God is for the religious fundamentalist who looks down their nose at you. God is for the worker who barely has time to rest, let alone contemplate the Divine. God is for the pagan who can't make heads or tails of this Jewish teacher and why everyone is so fascinated by him.

No matter what ways you have been told you are a failure, or how deeply you've internalized the narrative of the world around you, it is not true. The God of the universe is already on your side, cheering you on, because that's who God is. Blessed are you who don't have a clue, because the Divine has come near to you.

The Beatitudes are Jesus telling us about God. We've already talked about two of these eight sayings, but let's look at the full progression that leads us into Jesus' sermon proper: Blessed are the poor spirit, not because of who they are or anything they have to offer, but because the goodness of God comes to find them and welcomes them home. Next, we hear, "Blessed are those who mourn, for they will be comforted" (Matthew 5:4), which in the most basic sense is an implication of the first blessing. If the poor in spirit are welcomed, then of course those who mourn will be comforted when they arrive. However, this is also an expansion of the intent behind the first blessing.

Throughout human history, in Jesus' time and emphatically in ours, there has been an assumption that divine blessing brings with it material benefit: not solely wealth, but certainly that, and much more. Happiness, comfort, prosperity—all of these have been associated with the blessing of God in our imaginations. Jesus now flips all of that upside down by saying that blessing comes to find not only those who can't find our way back to God, but also those who mourn and grieve, including those of us who suffer from depression and can't seem to right ourselves on our own. The blessing of God is God's comforting presence with us, not the absence of the need to be comforted.

In other words, doing well is not a sign of God's favor. In fact, our struggle is the opportunity for God to draw near to us. Once again, we have to remember that this isn't about us, so no one should be looking to mourn just so that God will draw near. That's not the point Jesus is making. This is instead a statement about God and about whom God desires to be near to. This is Jesus teaching us about God's care-full-ness.

Blessed are the meek, for they will inherit the land they stand on, with all of the implications for power, merit, and justice we have already discussed. For God to welcome those who can't make sense of God, and for God to comfort those who have been afflicted, requires that God be invested in the righting of history. But now Jesus is on a roll.

Blessed are those who hunger and thirst for righteousness, for they will be filled. Often, we hear this as a challenge: we had better start working hard at being more righteous, being better religious persons. However, in light of the way this progression is unfolding, that interpretation seems to miss Jesus' point.

First of all, this word *righteousness* is actually just the word for justice. In Greek and in Hebrew, there is no difference between doing what is right religiously and doing what is right in the world. Truth is, it's in English where we use two different words to differentiate those contexts. (See Chapter Six for more discussion on this concept.) So, remember that every time you read *righteousness* instead of *justice* in your Bible, you are reading someone's interpretation of the context. In the end, however, you are reading a call to do what is right, period.

Jesus says that what is right is like something that grabs ahold of us from the inside and causes us to long for more of it. Rather than a thing to work our way toward, Jesus sees righteousness as a growing appetite. The more we see what is right, the more we understand what is right. The more we experience what is right, the more we desire what is right. The more we long for what is right in the world, the more we pursue what is right in the world around us, and we're thereby offered the chance to participate in a world here on earth that looks more like the one in heaven.

This is very much how grace seems to work for Jesus. It's in our poverty of spirit that God comes to us, telling us that we are loved and freeing us from the compulsion to be worthy of love. Then, this freedom allows us to begin to become the person all of our insecurities were stopping us from being in the first place. And that helps us to want new things.

Far from being heavy, this is Jesus showing us how God works. By grace we are saved, and by grace we are slowly and steadily transformed into the likeness of Christ. Once, we could barely even hope for a world that was better, but now that grace has met us in our poverty of spirit and opened us up to new possibilities, our ability to see the world in new ways begins to blossom and grow inside of us.

So remember this whenever you look around the world and see how things could be different, or how things could be more beautiful, or when you look inside and notice the areas where you still have growth to encounter. This is the blessing of God beginning to open you to new possibilities. And this process is why I'm convinced Jesus can be so confident that the merciful will be shown mercy. If grace comes to find us and helps us to hunger for a more just world, well then, it makes sense that for Jesus, the more we are shown mercy, the more merciful we will become. Once we get a sense that retribution is not how the world changes, then the only response is a virtuous cycle that draws us up and in and closer to the Divine heart.

Next comes, "Blessed are the pure in heart, for they will see God" (Matthew 5:8). I really like this one. However, it can be tough, because divorced from the preceding beatitudes, our first instinct is to return to that kind of task-list spirituality of which Jesus is trying to disabuse us. I think it's that word *pure*. It seems to have an unhealthy hold on us. It seems to want to draw us back into some kind measurement: "99.4-percent pure," just like a bar of soap, perhaps. Except that mindset works against everything Jesus has been inviting us into so far.

For me, it helps to put this beatitude into conversation with more of Jesus' thought. Later in this same Gospel, Jesus is really going after some of his contemporaries in a section called "the seven woes." He says, "Woe to you . . . . You clean the outside of the cup and dish, but inside they are full of greed and self-indulgence" (Matthew 23:25). First, clean the inside of the cup, and then the outside will be clean as well. This helps me to get a better handle on what I think Jesus is doing with this beatitude.

The idea here isn't that you have to be incredibly pure to see God. The idea is that if what you want out of life is to see God, you will. All of us mix motives and intentions at the best of times, but when it comes to religion, all of that complexity gets amplified. What do we want out of religion? Prestige? Reward? Admiration? I think this is a big theme for Jesus, and one he'll come back to later in the sermon. For now, though, as an introduction, what he's saying is not that you need to measure up in order to see God but that if you want to, you will. Pure in heart is simply about the focus of our desire and about the divine promise that God has always been looking for us.

"Blessed are the peacemakers, for they will be called children of God" (Matthew 5:9). All through the Hebrew Scriptures, indeed through most of human history, the guiding principle when it comes to peace has been the *lex talionis*, or the law of retaliation. In its simplest terms, this is the idea that the punishment must fit the crime—an eye for an eye and all that. This framework has allowed us to maintain some semblance of social order, but now Jesus goes one step further, past the containment of our violence toward the creation of real peace.

Later, Jesus will say that when an evil person slaps you, you should turn the other cheek. We'll explore the complexity of that teaching in detail in Chapter Four, but the roots of Jesus' imagination are planted here in the opening. Peacemaking, for Jesus, is part of our essential connectedness to God. All throughout Jesus' ministry, he will preach nonviolence, but in the climax of the Jesus story, he will do more than preserve the law of retaliation: he will make peace by absorbing our violence and giving us grace in return. Peacemaking is about more than the status quo; it is about the ways in which we imagine a world transformed by grace and then participate in its creation. In this, we are more than "like God"—we become family with God.

But now, finally, Jesus gets to transformation. After we have read each of these preceding beatitudes for what its illuminates about the Divine, Jesus brings us all the way back around to the beginning by talking about *us*. "Blessed are those who are persecuted because of righteousness, for theirs is the kingdom of heaven" (Matthew 5:10). And just like that, we're back where we started. Initially, Jesus told us that the kingdom of heaven was for those who could not make sense of God—those of us lost and confused and fumbling our way toward, or maybe even away from, God. Now the kingdom of heaven belongs to those who find themselves so captivated by the welcome, they give everything to it.

> Blessed are the poor in spirit, because God has come to find us.
> Blessed are those who mourn, because God is near to us.
> Blessed are the meek, because God will make all things right.
> Blessed are those who hunger for justice, because God will heal the world.
> Blessed are the merciful, because God is mercy.
> Blessed are the pure in heart, because God is willing to be found.
> Blessed are the peacemakers, because peace is our participation in God's family.

And now Jesus reminds us that those who are captivated by the way of Jesus are offered only the same blessing as those who couldn't even wrap their minds around blessing to begin with. This, I think, only makes sense once you are truly captured by the Way. For all of our lives, we are trained to believe that the reason we invest in something, the reason we give ourselves to something, is the reward. We think in transactions. But here Jesus says that in the end, the blessing of God that comes to find us and invites us to reimagine our world—that asks us to give our everything to it—offers us only the free gift that we always had, from the very first day. The mystery is that once you get there, it makes sense.

This is the brilliance of Jesus' way. He doesn't negotiate us into a better life with transactional thinking. He offers everything up front and trusts that if we really experience the gift of God, we will be changed by it.

The Beatitudes are Jesus' declaration of how the world could and should and will one day be, and the sooner we understand that it is all gift, the sooner we will embrace that grace that changes everything for us. And look, if we can get this, if we can sink it into our bones, it will change everything about us. It will open up new life inside of us. It will invite us to journey with Jesus and follow Jesus and sink into the teachings of Jesus. But it starts with who God is.

On the other hand, if we don't get this—if we don't get that we are already completely loved before we ever take a step—well, then, we will just keep trying harder to earn the love we already have, and the Divine will just seem farther and farther away. Because here's the thing about the Sermon on the Mount: if you don't get that God comes to you in your spiritual poverty, and loves you in your spiritual poverty, then you will read the rest of the Bible as the path to spiritual wealth, as rule after rule to live up to—and that is exactly the opposite of what Jesus is trying to say to you. Everything Jesus is about to say is predicated on the fact that the world is not what you think it is, love is not what you think it is, God is not who you think God is, and each of these is so much better than you could possibly imagine. You are already beloved of God.

Henri Nouwen is widely quoted as observing that the path of "theological formation is the gradual and often painful discovery of God's complete incomprehensibility" to you. In other words, you can be competent in many things, but you cannot be competent in God. And here Jesus begins his most famous sermon by saying that's all okay, for blessed are the spiritually incompetent. You don't need to do the right things, say the right things, know the right things, or believe the right things to have access to God's love, because God is near to you already, right now.

So, is Jesus saying that God loves you and God will continue to love you, even if you keep on being selfish, ignoring the Divine, following your own path, and disregarding God? The answer is absolutely, unequivocally, yes. You are loved. You will always be loved. You cannot do anything to make God love any more or any less, because you don't have the power to change God. But the thing is, once you know this—once Jesus gets through to you and gets into you, convincing you that you are not who you thought and you are not on your own—you will not, or cannot, remain the same person. It's not because you start to try harder; that's not the gospel. It's because real grace, which is the pure, unfettered divine love experienced in our lives, can't help but begin to transform us. Jesus says, "I don't need to tell you to be better. I need to tell you that you are loved, and if that lands, then everything else will begin to take care of itself."

In traditional Christian language, we say we are saved by grace, but sometimes, we forget that we are also sanctified by grace. It's not our best efforts that change us; it's God's love that transforms us. And that's why, if you heard Jesus saying that you are loved already, as you are, and your first thought was, "Great, I can go on with my life, stealing and abusing and mistreating those around me," then I'm telling you, you did not hear Jesus. What you heard was your own greed justifying itself, but you did not hear this divine love that changes everything in us. This disconnect is what makes the gospel so elusive.

God says, "You are loved," and we somehow struggle to turn that into either a license to be jerks or something to live up to, and neither of those responses truly comprehends grace. So Jesus says, "No, no, no, let's start again. You are loved all the way to the cross and back, because love is the only thing that can turn our worst moments into something beautiful."

Amid all of the anxiety and expectations that school and work and family place on us every day, and all of the pressure we feel obliged to measure up to, perhaps start by learning to sink into your spiritual poverty. Embrace the truth that you never measured up but that this never made a difference to God. Because God's love is like nothing you have ever experienced before.

May you know yourself as God knows you today—as blessed and beloved, as welcomed and accepted, as invited into everything you might become if only you could see yourself as beautifully as God sees you right now. Blessed are you, poor in spirit, for the kingdom of God has come to you.

WORKBOOK

Chapter One Journal

Journal Prompt: Reflect on this definition of poor in spirit: *Simply put, it means complete confusion when it comes to the things of God. In other words, blessed are you who have no clue.* Take a moment to sit with this potentially new definition of the phrase. How does it compare to how you understood its meaning prior to reading this book? What kind of response or feelings toward God does it elicit? How does it change or confirm your understanding of God's love for you and others?

_____

_____

_____

_____

_____

_____

_____

_____

_____

_____

_____

_____

_____

_____

CHAPTER TWO

Salt and Light

The writer of the Gospel of Matthew goes out of his way to tell us who's in the audience: it is rural Jews trying to do their best under an oppressive regime. It's religious elites from Jerusalem who broker the power and politics of religion. It is the Greek and Roman pagans from Decapolis who have their own religions but are considered godless by their Jewish contemporaries. In fact, Matthew 4:25 describes this crowd using the term *óchlos*[11] *polýs*,[12] which refers to a throng or mass of people, but with implications of a rabble—that is, the unwashed, unfiltered masses. That's who's here to listen to what Jesus has to say.

Dallas Willard, in his book *The Divine Conspiracy*, writes, "Standing around Jesus as he speaks are people with no spiritual qualifications or abilities at all. You would never call on them when 'spiritual work' is to be done. There is nothing about them to suggest that the breath of God might move through their lives. They have no charisma, no religious glitter or clout."[13] In fact, these people would be the first to tell you they really can't make heads or tails of religion.

And to the crowd, to this mishmash of humanity—rural Jews, religious fundamentalists, and non-Jews with completely different assumptions about God—Jesus begins by telling them that all those who can't make sense of God are blessed. For God has come to find you.

WHAT IS RIGHT

> *Blessed are you when people insult you, persecute you and falsely say all kinds of evil against you because of me. Rejoice and be glad, because great is your reward in heaven, for in the same way they persecuted the prophets who were before you.*
>
> *You are the salt of the earth. But if the salt loses its saltiness, how can it be made salty again? It is no longer good for anything, except to be thrown out and trampled underfoot.*
>
> *You are the light of the world. A town built on a hill cannot be hidden. Neither do people light a lamp and put it under a bowl. Instead they put it on its stand, and it gives light to everyone in the house. In the same way, let your light shine before others, that they may see your good deeds and glorify your Father in heaven.*
> —*Matthew 5:11–16*

Jesus ends the Beatitudes by saying, "Blessed are those who are persecuted because of righteousness, for theirs is the kingdom of heaven" (Matthew 5:10), which, by the way, is the same gift given to the poor of spirit in the first Beatitude. The result is a nice *inclusio*, wherein the speaker or writer reinforces the theme under discussion with a statement of the main idea at both the beginning and the end. Jesus has got skills.

Our assumption here, based on the Beatitudes, is that Jesus is not now giving us a task list to live up to. Instead, he's beginning to describe the life that emerges from within us as God's grace and love begin to take root in us. The kingdom of heaven is gifted to all of us, but the kingdom of heaven is also what transforms us from poverty of spirit toward becoming righteous actors in the world. And from there, Jesus expands this description by saying, "Blessed are you when people insult you, persecute you and falsely say all kinds of evil against you because of me."

Now, important piece here: you are not blessed, and God is not impressed, when people avoid you because you are belligerent. That is not what Jesus is talking about here. Yet there are all kinds of voices who seem to think that their proficiency in annoying people with religion is somehow a badge of honor. It's not. People did not hate Jesus; the people loved Jesus, as evidenced by the huge crowds that gathered to listen to him. The ones who hated Jesus, the ones who persecuted him, were the ones who were threatened by him.

And this is the key here: Jesus says, "Blessed are those who are persecuted because of righteousness" (Matthew 5:10). It's not because of *your* righteousness; it's *dediōgmenoi heneken dikaiosynēs*,[14] which means "the quality, state, or practice of judicial responsibility [with] focus on fairness, *justice, equitableness, fairness.*" The word *dikaiosynēs* is the Greek word that corresponds to the Hebrew word *tsadaq*, which means "brought to its justice"[15] and is an incredibly important word in the Hebrew Scriptures.

In the Hebrew Scriptures, the idea of an internal, personal rightness with God was not separate or distinct from an external, corporate rightness in the world. And so, in Hebrew, they don't have separate words for righteousness and justice. They are the same thing, encompassing what is right.

Also notice here that there is no "your." There is nothing to personalize Jesus' statement. It's not *your* righteousness for which you are being persecuted and blessed, so we would probably better read it, "Blessed are those who are persecuted because of what is right between us in the world." We tend to call that justice.

This blessing, and this persecution, of which Jesus speaks do not come to those who huddle together in their religious enclaves. It is for those who do what is right for others, even at great cost to themselves. In other words, you do not get a star for looking out for yourself. You do not need divine love for that. No, you are blessed when God's love moves in and through you and you realize that this love needs to find expression in the world for those who don't have it yet.

If that's your story—if you are working on behalf of the powerless, the voiceless, and the marginalized—well, then, you are going to challenge the status quo, and that is going to upset people. One of the really interesting things in the Gospels is watching the poor and the oppressed immediately seize on the significance of Jesus' message, this good news that has come to them. But then, as the story unfolds, we watch those in power slowly turn the masses into mobs. And their discontent is mobilized into anger, which is then weaponized against Jesus, until Jesus is scapegoated by those he is working hard to save.

The key here is to recognize that the persecution Jesus speaks of comes not when we defend ourselves, our religion, and our way of life. In fact, we're called to give all of that away, anyway. It comes when we learn to work for those who don't have what we take for granted, because as Jesus says, that is what the prophets were always all about.

SALT: FLAVORFUL PRESERVATIVE

Next, Jesus transitions from the blessing of God that comes to us, on the one hand, to the life that blessing begins to inspire in us, on the other. For that, he uses two metaphors: salt and light.

I love salt. I keep a collection of different salts in my house for different culinary applications. I put salt on everything: on pasta, on pizza, on sandwiches, on ice cream, on cookies, on watermelon. The reason I love salt is not just because of that delicious sodium fix; it's because salt brings out the flavors around it. We have salt, sour, sweet, bitter, and umami taste receptors, and salt is able to heighten those other flavors. It's why putting a bit of salt on your watermelon will make it taste sweeter. I promise.

But this knowledge is not new; it is as old as this text. In fact, the ancient Hebrew writer Ben Sirach says, "The basic necessities of human life are water and fire and iron and salt and wheat flour and milk and honey, the blood of the grape and oil and clothing. All these are good for the godly" (Sirach 39:26–27a).[16]

And old Ben Sirach is right. Salt has been celebrated throughout human history for two main purposes: to make everything taste better and to preserve food. I think both of those ideas are present here in Jesus' imagination. You are the salt of the earth. You are here to make all things taste better, and you are here to preserve what is already good within all things.

So, what does that mean? Let's look back to the Beatitudes. Jesus says, "Blessed are those who hunger and thirst for righteousness, for they will be filled" (Matthew 5:6). This is another culinary-based metaphor. Those who hunger and thirst are those who want to see what is right in the world and in themselves, but they hunger and they thirst because they don't quite see it yet. And to them Jesus says, "You are blessed before you ever measure up, you are blessed before you ever take a step, and you are blessed the moment you begin to imagine a world that is better than the one you see around you right now."

Know this: your imagination, or the way you see the world and know it could be better, and desire to see it made so—the way you dream about a world that is more equitable, more generous, more beautiful, more gracious, more of what you already know is good and sacred and life-giving—is in itself a blessing. Because that dissatisfaction, when channeled appropriately, puts you in touch with the way the world could be, should be, and will be one day. Jesus says that you are not a dreamer; you are ahead of the curve.

But here he says, "You are the salt of the earth. You are here to notice where the flavor is lacking, and you are here to make it all taste better. That hungering and that thirsting, that awareness of opportunity around you, is blessing, but part of the blessing is that it's also part of discovering your purpose. You hunger for a world that tastes better and then start seasoning it with the flavors you are uniquely designed to bring to the table."

And look, I know I'm really driving this flavor metaphor here, but I really love it because Jesus isn't asking us all to start over. He's not asking everyone to be a revolutionary or lead some massive social change. I think he's saying, if you can imagine something different, if you can see where things could be better, you can begin right now in small ways to shift the flavors of the world around you. He's saying kindness will go further than you think it will and generosity will stretch further than your bank account. So will putting yourself in someone else's shoes, listening to their story, and honoring their journey even if it doesn't sound like yours. Conversations with neighbors, smiles for strangers, unnecessary compliments—all of these really will change the world, one pinch at a time.

Now, I'm not saying that's all we need. We do need revolutionaries and sweeping change, and we do need an imagination for a world completely reinvented by grace. But not all of us are called to lead movements. Some of us are called to help our slice of the world taste better right now. And all of that is sacred and holy before God.

The ancients knew about how delicious salt was, but they also knew how powerful salt was. Numbers 18:19 says: "Whatever is set aside from the holy offerings the Israelites present to the Lord I give to you and your sons and daughters as your perpetual share. It is an everlasting covenant of salt before the Lord for both you and your offspring." And Leviticus 2:13 says: "Season all your grain offerings with salt. Do not leave the salt of the covenant of your God out of your grain offerings; add salt to all your offerings."

This wasn't just an Israelite thing, either. In Babylon, they would refer to their allies as those who had tasted the salt of the tribe.[17] And in Persia, swearing loyalty to the king was said to be "tasting the salt of the palace" (Ezra 4:14).[18] In fact, in Aramaic, the word for *treaty* or *agreement* is a form of the verb *to salt*.[19] So, what's going on with all of these salt covenants?

Well, in the ancient world, salt was the primary way anything was preserved. Salt became, across all of these cultures, a metaphor for any promise, agreement, covenant, or treaty that could never go bad, dissolve, or become void. Essentially, your salt was your signature. It meant that your word was good for something.

When God used salt in God's promises to the world, this was God using the images of the ancient world to say that God will not let us down. God's promise is trustworthy and dependable and forever. And so, when Jesus comes along and says that *you* are the salt of the earth, part of what he's saying is that you are here to be proof of God's promise, fidelity, and never-ending commitment to the world. You are God's signature on the deal.

What does that mean? It means that you and I, and those who sat on the side of a mountain some two thousand years ago to listen to Jesus—all of us who have attempted in our broken, confused, sometimes misguided attempts to follow the path of God in the world—are proof to the world that God still cares. God's promise, and God's word, and God's investment in the world are embodied in those of us who are here seasoning the world, preparing the world, and reminding the world that the story is not yet done.

WHAT ILLUMINATES OUR WAY

Jesus says that you are the salt of the earth and the light of the world. In English, that kind of rolls off the tongue without much thought. *Earth* and *world* are pretty synonymous for us, but in the Greek, there is a meaningful distinction here.

Earth here is the word *gē*.[20] It's literally the stuff that you walk on, the earth beneath you. *World*, on the other hand, is the word *kosmos* in Greek, and they use that a little differently than we do. It didn't necessarily mean the stars and galaxies and solar systems we take for granted today, but it was much more than the earth. The *kosmos* was everything in the earth and everything on the earth. It is defined as "the sum total of everything here and now, *the world, the (orderly) universe*."[21] It was all the systems and the structures.[22] The apostle Paul uses the words "principalities" and "powers" (Ephesians 6:12) to talk about religion, politics, economics, and everything that shapes our experience of the earth. All of that was bound up in this word *kosmos*.

So, when Jesus says that we are the salt of the ground and we are the light of the cosmos, he is saying that our commitment to the story of God runs the gamut from the dirt we till to grow our food to the systems and structures that define our relationships to everything and everyone around us. This encompasses sustainable food production, equitable economic systems, healthy concepts of neighbor, and opposition to patriarchy and white supremacy. It includes small moments of kindness as well as large-scale justice initiatives that balance the scales of the world. All of these exist on a continuum for Jesus. They are not either/or; they are both/and. You are the salt of the ground beneath you, *and* you are the light of the cosmos above you. You are part of what is good about both dirt and stardust.

With this in mind, don't despise small moments of generosity. The smallest act you take is beautiful before God. Yet, at the same time, don't be surprised when a few small acts of beauty turn into a life of purpose and a commitment to change the world in ways you can't even begin to imagine right now. There is far more in you than you realize, but it starts on the ground beneath you. When you see beauty and celebrate it by helping someone else see what is beautiful all around them, you are the salt that preserves the best of God's world. And when you see injustice and stand for what is right—when you work to return the world to the rhythms of love God embedded in the universe—you are the salt that preserves the best of God's world. When you extend yourself beyond yourself, growing your circle to include the person who is convinced that they have been forgotten, and you remind them that their story is important to you, you are the salt.

But here's the real beauty of it: you don't need to create the best of God's world; you don't need to dream it up. You simply need to become aware of all the goodness already embedded in God's creation all around you. Because the salt isn't the main course. Salt is what preserves, points to, seasons, and elevates all of the goodness God is already doing all around us all the time. And this is what is so remarkable about Jesus. He is a member of a marginalized group of people from a conquered country, who has no land or wealth to speak of, and yet he does not see the world as irretrievably damaged. For Jesus, the world is indescribably beautiful and filled with potential, infused with sacred purpose just below the grit, grime, blood, sweat, and tears that obscure our imagination of everything that could be.

If that's what you see in the world, too—not a knackered world intended for Gehenna, but a beautiful world marred by sin—well, then, of course you want to season it. Of course you want to preserve the best of it. Of course you want to lean in instead of backing away from it. Of course you want to let the light that's growing within you shine before others, because no one lights a lamp just to put it under a bowl.

This is not Jesus telling you to go buy a placard and stand downtown with a megaphone yelling at people; this is Jesus talking about the natural, normal, instinctive response to good news that fills us with joy for what is and hope for what could be. That response is to let the light leak out.

Salt and light are not something to live up to. Salt and light are the life that is in you right now, waiting to be unleashed in the world.

WORKBOOK

Chapter Two Journal

Journal Prompt: Reflect on the definition of *salt* in this chapter: *Salt is what preserves, points to, seasons, and elevates all of the goodness God is already doing all around us all the time.* Think about the ways you are doing this already. What are your dreams? What are the ways in which you envision the world becoming even more beautiful? What is the unique flavor you bring to the world?

_____

_____

_____

_____

_____

_____

_____

_____

_____

_____

_____

_____

_____

_____

CHAPTER THREE

Turning the Law on Its Head

Whenever I talk about the Beatitudes, and whenever I get going on grace, inevitably someone will ask me about truth and law and justice and all that serious stuff, as if there is some kind of contradiction. It seems to me that Jesus is similarly confronted, in which I take little bit of solace. However, far from running from those questions, Jesus turns to face them directly.

After welcoming us into this new imagination of reality we call the Beatitudes, and after talking about the life this imagination lights inside of us, Jesus now turns directly to answer those who might feel his picture of God is perhaps just a little bit too rosy. Which, by the way, is always an indictment of our lack of imagination. If your God is not better than you can imagine, you really do have a problem.

THE WHIPLASH

Let's start by reading Matthew 5:17, when Jesus says, "Do not think that I have come to abolish the Law or the Prophets." If Jesus begins with that statement, it should tell us something about his audience.

It should tell us that some people think he is here to abolish the law and the prophets. In other words, the tension between Jesus' interpretation of the law and the religious status quo is obvious to everyone in the crowd, and to miss that is to miss a big part of the story. If you have ever thought the Good News was scandalous, well, so does everyone else listening to Jesus' sermon.

> *Do not think that I have come to abolish the Law and the Prophets; I have not come to abolish them but to fulfill them. For truly I tell you, until heaven and earth disappear [which is another way of saying it's not going to happen], not the smallest letter, not the least stroke of a pen, [this is that famous "jot and tittle" in the King James] will by any means disappear from the Law until everything is accomplished.*
> —*Matthew 5:17-18*

Step back for a second and imagine this scene: Jesus begins this section by saying, "I know what I'm saying flies in the face of everything you've been told to believe. I know everything I'm telling you sounds too good to true. I know some of you, right now, are fuming in your tunics as you listen to me, but follow me on this one. The law is not going anywhere, because the law has divine purpose."

And then, just as those in the crowd—who have been shocked by what they've heard—are perking up and pulling their eyes away from their ancient smartphones, and the ancient nasty #heretic tweets they are about to post, Jesus adds:

> *You have heard that it was said to the people long ago, "You shall not murder, and anyone who murders will be subject to judgment." But I tell you that anyone who is angry with a brother or sister will be subject to judgment . . . .*
>
> *You have heard that it was said, "You shall not commit adultery." But I tell you that anyone who looks at a woman lustfully has already committed adultery with her in his heart . . . .*
>
> *Again, you have heard that it was said to the people long ago, "Do not break your oath, but fulfill to the Lord the vows you have made." But I tell you, do not swear an*

> oath at all: either by heaven, for it is God's throne; or by the
> earth, for it's God's footstool; or by Jerusalem, for it is the
> city of the Great King. And do not swear by your head, for
> you cannot make even one hair white or black.
> —*Matthew 5:21-22, 27-28, 33-36*

Jesus also says, "You have heard that it was said, 'Eye for eye, and tooth for tooth.' But I tell you, do not resist an evil person" (Matthew 5:38–39a). And he adds, "You have heard that it was said, 'Love your neighbor and hate your enemy.' But I tell you, love your enemies and pray for those who persecute you" (Matthew 5:33–34).

Now, understand how incredibly strange this all is. Jesus begins to teach a random crowd about God. Some in the audience think it's profound and beautiful. Others likely think it is dangerous and heretical, as if Jesus were throwing out centuries of religious law that has guided the community. Jesus says, "Actually, no, that's not the case." In fact, he says, "I love the law. I'm here to complete the law, to accomplish the law. I want to bring the law to its ultimate goal." And then he proceeds to quote various laws and redefine them

Now, that's some whiplash.

THE TWO TORAHS

To understand what Jesus is saying here, we've got to understand a few things about how Jewish people thought about some of the terms involved. As Christians, we are very used to hearing "law" and thinking of our Old Testament, but that is not exactly what a Jewish person thinks about.

In the culture surrounding Jesus, *Torah*, or law, came in two flavors: there was *Torah shebictav*, which meant the written law. This was the first five books of your Bible: Genesis, Exodus, Leviticus, Numbers, and Deuteronomy. (And by the way, when Jesus talks about "the Law and the Prophets," that is a shorthand way of including the rest of the Hebrew Scriptures as well, which is the Tanakh today).

But when it came to law, there was also *Torah she-beal peh*, or the oral law—literally, "Torah in the mouth."[23] And so, when Jesus talks about the *Torah* or law, he really has both of these in mind.

Now, the written kind of Torah has 613 rules. There are 365 prohibitions, or things you shouldn't do—one for every day, except on a leap year. And there are 248 impositions, or things you must do as a follower of YHWH.[24] That might sound like a lot of rules, but of course, it still couldn't adjudicate every possible permutation. So the oral law was all of the interpretation that followed: what it meant to follow the rules, how you follow the rules, when and where and what to do to keep the rules in all of the complexity of the real world.

In the Jewish culture, *Torah shebictav* was understood to be incomplete without *Torah she-be'al peh*. After all, a rule isn't meaningful until it's implemented. The *Torah she-be'al peh* stayed oral for almost all of ancient history—until, incidentally, around the time that the New Testament was being put together. In the fourth century, Jewish leaders began gathering all of the teachings of all of the great interpreters, and those become the Talmud.

However, at the time of Jesus, the Torah is still the written law *and* the spoken law. The law is the rules plus their interpretation, and so, when Jesus says, "You have heard it said . . . but I tell you . . . ," what he is doing is giving the written law *and* his oral law.

For example, in the written law, there was a rule saying that in order to enter the temple, to bring sacrifices to God, you had to be ritually clean. And that meant you could not enter the temple within seven days of touching a dead body or touching blood that wasn't your own. For priests, there was even a law forbidding them from approaching a dead body (Ezekiel 44:25) and an interpretation suggesting that they should not even walk beneath the branches of a tree whose branches extend over a dead body.[25]

So, when Jesus tells a story about a man who was lying in a ditch after being beaten by robbers, and Jesus says that a priest crossed over to the other side of the road to pass by, it could be that this priest was attempting to fulfill the oral law. We should note, however, that a close reading of the text in Luke tells us the priest was "going down the same road" (Luke 10:31) as the man who was injured which likely indicates he, too, was leaving Jerusalem, in which case, ritual purity would not have been his concern. In fact, the Jewish principle of *Pikuach nefesh*, which taught that any action to save a human life took precedence over religious prohibitions, would have overridden any pious concerns, regardless.[26]

But that's the point. The Good Samaritan story, with its repeated examples of respectable characters avoiding the responsibility to help a Samaritan victim, isn't a critique of Jewish law. It's an example of Jesus challenging expectations and providing a new oral law to live by, one that says kindness takes precedence over appearances—a very Jewish idea to be sure. You can fulfill the law by breaking the law to follow a better way. This approach puts Jesus right smack in the middle of probably the definitive oral law controversy of his time, showing just how malleable the law was.

SHAMMAI AND HILLEL

In the years before Jesus, two very famous Jewish teachers emerged, whose teachings became known as the house of Hillel and the house of Shammai. There's a story that is probably apocryphal, but it helps illustrate the difference between their two approaches.[27]

It's said that a young gentile, or non-Jewish, man once came to the teacher Shammai. And depending on who is telling the story, he was either earnest in his inquiry or simply mocking the extensive rule-keeping in Judaism. But he came to Shammai while the latter was instructing his disciples and said to the teacher, "If you can explain your law to me while I stand on one foot, I will convert on the spot and worship your God for the rest of my life."

Well, the teacher Shammai was deeply insulted by this. He yelled at the man, "You do not understand God. Not one yod or qotz can be removed from the Torah." And he chased the man off his step.

The man, having been chased away by Shammai, was perhaps emboldened in his trolling, and he tracked down the other most famous rabbi in town, Hillel, and did the same thing. He showed up while Hillel was teaching his students. He crashed the class and said, "If you can explain your law to me while I stand on one foot, I will convert on the spot and worship your God for the rest of my life."

Hillel looked up from his students, paused, and said, "What you dislike, do not do to your friend. The rest is commentary, so go and learn." And then he returned to his lesson. Well, the young man was speechless, so the story goes, and without a word, he quietly sat among the students and devoted the rest of his life to learning the law.

Now, clearly that story was told by a student of Hillel. It's obviously not meant to make Shammai the hero. But this story illustrates well the central tenant of Hillel's approach to the Torah: it was called the law of reciprocity, the shorthand for which became, "What is distasteful to you, do not do to another."

Of course, Jesus will take this formulation and flip it on its head. He will transform the law of reciprocity into the law of love by saying, "Not only should you avoid what is hurtful, but you should also pursue—go out of your way—to do what is good for another. Don't just avoid what you wouldn't want; do what you *do* want for your neighbor." In other words, it's not what you don't do that makes you righteous. Righteousness is an active posture that entails a disposition toward the good.

But around the time of Jesus, these two teachers and their respective houses, Shammai and Hillel, became synonymous with how you approached the law. Either laws are laws because laws are laws, so you fulfill the law by following the law, or laws are part of a story, in which case, all laws are important but some laws take precedence. So start with the most important ones and work your way out from there.

Today, if you want to pigeonhole someone and skip the hard work of understanding them as a human being, you might ask, "Are you a liberal or a conservative?" In Jesus' day, you might ask, "Are you party to the house of Hillel, or do you follow the house of Shammai?" Except that Jesus somehow continually finds ways to sidestep those binaries. And here in the Sermon on the Mount, he begins with divine love and the grace of God that is out there in the world looking for us, chasing us down. He moves to the life that love creates inside of us, and the flavor and the light that bleed out of us when we let God in.

But then, it's almost as if he can see it on people's faces. He can see them struggling to make sense of him, to categorize him, to figure out which box to put him in, and so he says, "Do not think I have come to abolish the law, not one *yod* or *qotz*, not one jot or tittle, not the smallest mark will fall away, for I understand the house of Shammai." And just as those people are trying to make sense of that, and figure out how he fits in that box, he says, "No, I'm not here to destroy anything. I'm here to bring the law, finally, to life."

Now, imagine you are sitting in the crowd. You are amazed by what he says, but you are confused about what box to put him in. And now he says that all of it matters, even the smallest stroke, precisely because the law is not yet full. Whether you follow Hillel or Shammai—whether you are conservative or liberal, a traditionalist or a revolutionary—if you want to put Jesus in a nice, tidy box, then all of a sudden, you are a little bit lost.

For Jesus, every word of the story has meaning. But those who wield the words of God's story as a weapon, imposing them without compassion, have somehow missed that meaning completely. In fact, later in this same Gospel, Jesus will challenge the religious leaders and say that those who sit in the seat of Moses—in other words, those who adjudicate the law—tie up heavy, cumbersome loads and put them on other people's shoulders, yet they themselves are not willing to lift a finger to help (Matthew 23:2–4). And that is not, nor can it ever be, good news.

Every jot of the law matters, but every jot matters not so you can quote it at people; instead, it's so that you can understand where God has been with us and, through that, begin to imagine where the story is headed. Then, you can fulfill the law even if it means breaking it.

WHAT THE LAW IS REALLY FOR

The language of fulfilling and abolishing is really important to what's happening here. In Jewish midrash, there's a story that says that King Solomon once had the text of Deuteronomy 17:17 edited to give himself license. By removing one letter, a *yod*, the king changed the meaning of a word and removed the prohibition on polygamy, thus allowing himself to marry as many women as he wanted to. And so, in Jewish literature, the story goes:

> *Our Sages said, that at that time, the little yod (י) from the word yarbeh (הברי) ascended on high and prostrated itself before the Holy One, and said: "Master of the Universe! Did you not say that no letter shall ever be abolished from the Torah? Behold, now Solomon has arisen and abolished me. Who knows? Today he has abolished one letter, tomorrow he will abolish another—until the whole Torah be abolished!"*
>
> *And the Holy One, replied: "Solomon and a thousand like him will pass away, but the smallest mark will not be abolished."*
> **—Exodus Rabbah 6.1**[28]

What we see in these stories are examples of how these terms *abolish* and *fulfill* had become synonyms for either understanding it or completely missing the point.

If you take just one letter out and that changes the meaning, it's like you've abolished the whole thing. But if, on the other hand, you understand the story so well that you begin to live out of it with your full being, it's like you have fulfilled the entirety of it.

Here Jesus says, "I've not come to abolish it. Every jot matters. I've come to fulfill it. Everything needs to be continually contextualized." And that's why the next thing he does after affirming his commitment to every jot is completely reinterpret the Torah.

"You have heard that it was said, 'You shall not murder,' but I tell that's not enough. You have heard that it was said, 'You shall not commit adultery,' but I tell you that's just a start. You have heard that it was said, 'Eye for eye, and tooth for tooth,' but I tell you, we have to learn to grow beyond all of that now."

In other words, for Jesus, abolishing the law was about missing the point, getting stuck on the jots and refusing to move in concert with God, whereas fulfilling the law was always about understanding exactly where the jots were pointing and learning to move together with them.

Even when Jesus veers into what can be heard as strict moralizing, teaching about lust and divorce, his ideas are rooted in the trajectory of Scripture. As any young man growing up in the church knows, Jesus says that "anyone who looks at a woman lustfully has already committed adultery with her in his heart" (Matthew 5:28). However, where we read "lustfully" in our Bibles, the Greek text of Matthew uses *epithymeō*. Now, it's true that in Greek usage, this word held a strong connotation of sexual desire[29], but it's also the word used in the Septuagint to translate "covet" in Exodus 20:17. There the commandment says, "you shall not covet your neighbor's house. You shall not covet your neighbor's wife, or his male or female servant, his ox or donkey, or anything that belongs to your neighbor." Here, Jesus is not condemning healthy sexual desire or even the fact we may notice each other as sexually attractive. He is warning us of the danger in allowing our sexuality to turn another human being into a piece of property to acquire. Sexual desire is a gift, but it can lead us to dehumanize each other if we're not careful with it. Jesus sees recognizing each other as fully human, even in our sexuality, as part of the fulfillment of the 10th commandment.

And by the way, Jesus puts the remedy for such moments squarely on those who struggle to see the object of their desire as fully human. As many have pointed out, Jesus believes that men are capable of taking radical action to correct their unhealthy patterns rather than expecting women to do that work for them (Matthew 5:29–30). Ironically, expecting women to dress in ways to accommodate men may, in fact, be closer to the kind of property-based covetousness that Jesus warns us against here. She is not *yours* to direct.

Jesus' ideas about divorce follow a similar pattern. "It has been said, 'Anyone who divorces his wife must give her a certificate of divorce.' But I tell you that anyone who divorces his wife, except for sexual immorality, makes her the victim of adultery" (Matthew 5:31–32). The context here is Deuteronomy 24:1 where a man who sends his wife away is instructed to give her a "certificate of divorce". That certificate was necessary in a patriarchal society where women had little access to personal wealth, could be sent away for almost any reason, and had no grounds to initiate a divorce themselves. For lack of a better term, it allowed them to re-enter the dating pool and find a new spouse to care for them. As Jesus explains later, divorce was always a concession to the hardness of men's hearts (Matthew 19:8), but in that concession, the vulnerability of the divorced partner was at least somewhat protected. Now Jesus clarifies that this bare minimum was never a fulfillment of the full intent of the law and that the practice of divorce for socially acceptable reasons as trivial as the spoiling of a meal[30] made the divorced partner a victim of the same kind of dehumanizing practices that our covetousness can create.

In all these examples, Jesus demonstrates how mere adherence to the law can undermine the intent of the law in our lives. Our fulfillment of law requires us to imagine how the story has unfolded and continually question what it might challenge next.

N. T. Wright uses the metaphor of acts in a play to explain this. He says that Scripture is authoritative the way the first few acts of a play are.[31] You can't possibly write the final act faithfully without understanding everything that has come before, every jot and tittle. But you don't write the last act of your play by copying the previous acts. No, you write it by allowing everything that has come before—every word, every story, every beautiful, difficult, messy moment in God's tale—to inform and shape and point you toward the life that God is asking you to live right now.

Jesus makes clear he has not come to destroy anything, but to show you what all of it actually looks like when it finally, fully comes to life in the world. "You've heard it said, don't murder. I tell you, that story ends in the pursuit of peace. You've heard it said, don't commit adultery. I tell you, that story ends when people aren't objects anymore. You've heard it said, don't break your oath. I tell you, that story ends when your actions speak for themselves.

You've heard, 'An eye for an eye,' but I say, retribution is overrated. You've heard, 'Hate your enemy.' I tell you, that one's been done, and trust me, it's not good news."

Because for Jesus, the law wasn't an end in itself. The law was a story, and that story was designed to make us more like him. And if it doesn't—if the law doesn't make you more kind, more gracious, more loving, more Jesus-y—well, then, it doesn't matter where that law came from, how long it's been around, or who taught it to you. It needs to be rethought in the light of Christ, because beneath every law is a good that God is orienting us toward.

If we confuse the law as being identical to the good, and so we forsake the good to follow the law, our story won't end up looking like Jesus and we will have missed the point. This is why, in the end, understanding how Jesus thinks about law is even more important than understanding how Jesus interprets any particular law. The truth is, we don't live in Jesus' time and culture, yet it's all okay because Jesus is with us, beside us, helping us make his story our story today.

And so, at the end of the day, the question that faces us will not be, "Did we get it all right?" Because for anyone who is honest with themselves, of course, the answer is no. Instead, the questions that face those of us who follow Jesus are: "Did we allow ourselves to become malleable and teachable? Were we responsive and open? Did we listen for God's spirit, and when we heard God's spirit speak, did we receive God's grace and allow it to change us? Did we come to know ourselves as loved, and did we let that love shape us as it was intended to?" If that becomes our story, then no matter how badly we mess up the law, Christ will still somehow fulfill all of it within us.

Love God with everything you have. Love your neighbor as yourself. All the law and the prophets hang on these. Because rules for rules' sake will rule over you and never change you. But a story that becomes you will welcome you into God's kingdom that continues to unfold to this day.

WORKBOOK

Chapter Three Journal

Journal Prompt: Reflect on how Jesus shook up the right way to approach the law: *You actually fulfill the law by breaking the law to follow a better law.* How does that idea sit with you? Are you a by-the-book rule follower? How do you feel at the thought of law being hierarchical? Have you ever weaponized God's word or wielded it without compassion? How does what Jesus says in his Sermon on the Mount challenge how you have approached others with God's word?

_____

_____

_____

_____

_____

_____

_____

_____

_____

_____

_____

_____

_____

CHAPTER FOUR

You Have Heard It Said

IN THE LAST CHAPTER, we talked about the way Jesus invites us to go beyond the letter of the law and instead to embody the intent behind the law. This is, of course, much easier said than done. In fact, it will take more than a lifetime to master, but Jesus now dives right into one of his most famous and perplexing examples of his way in the world.

There are a couple things to keep in mind here as we dive in. First of all, Jesus begins with one of his favorite phrases: "You have heard that it was said." And what we have to understand is that when Jesus says this, he's not just talking about well-known phrases or common-sense ideas—He's actually quoting from the Hebrew scriptures.

In this case, "eye for eye, and tooth for tooth" comes from several places in the Torah (Exodus 21, Leviticus 24, Deuteronomy 19). However, the concept predates all of that. The code of Hammurabi, an ancient Mesopotamian document from roughly 3,800 years ago, uses these same phrases,[32] and the lex talionis, or law of retaliation as it came it be known, was intended—as in the Bible—to limit the escalation of revenge. We're not creating peace *per se*, as Jesus invites us to in the Beatitudes, but we are at least keeping what little peace we may have.

That said, you may read these words and notice the inherent violence in them. Do we really want to be endorsing the gouging of eyes and chopping of hands in the pursuit of revenge? The problem with that approach is that it misses the nuance with which these texts were used in the ancient world. For example, the second-century student of Rabbi Akivva, Rabbi Simeon ben Yohai, says, "Eye for eye means monetary compensation."[33] What he means by this is that the point was never to inflict revenge on the antagonist but to compensate the victim for their loss. And, far from being an outlier, this was the standard interpretation in many schools.

The rabbis thus understood this as figurative language, speaking about recompense and not the literal gouging of eyes. In fact, nowhere in the Bible, or in Hebrew history, do we see these passages applied literally. So, for lack of a better parallel, this was an ancient form of long-term disability, similar in concept to how my insurance will place a dollar figure on the loss of my hand.

Taken together, this context helps us understand that the lex talionis is not a violent fantasy Jesus works to overturn but, instead, is a barrier to violent escalation on which Jesus expands. The escalation of revenge is a topic the Bible knows a lot about.

A DONKEY'S JAWBONE

One of the stories you may have heard as a kid is the story of Samson. However, a lot of us are unaware of the fact that Samson's story starts way back before Delilah betrays him and his long, luscious hair.

It's in Judges 14 that we find the story of Samson. There he, a Hebrew man, falls for a Philistine woman—forbidden love and all that—and decides he wants to marry her. Of course, his parents object. They want him to find a nice Jewish girl (Judges 14:3), but he says, "No, this is one I love. I've made up my mind," and everyone eventually agrees. So they have this big festival to celebrate the pending nuptials (Judges 14:10), and Samson's parents and his new family are there.

But during the party, Samson decides to make a bet with some of his new in-laws. He gives them a riddle: "Out of the eater, something to eat; out of the strong, something sweet" (Judges 14:14). "If you can solve this before the wedding," he says, "which is coming up in seven days, I'll give you thirty fancy linen outfits. However, if you can't solve it, then you have to give me thirty fancy linen outfits" (Judges 14:12–13, paraphrased).

Now, the problem here is that the "riddle" isn't so much a riddle as an inside joke. Once, Samson killed a lion, and later on, when he walked by the dead animal, he saw some bees building a nest in the carcass. He ate the honey and, apparently, came up with this riddle (Judges 14:5–9). However, because it's based entirely on his own personal experience, there's no way anyone could solve it. Well, when these future brothers-in-law can't figure it out, they go to their sister and say, "Listen, you have to help us here. We don't have thirty fancy linen outfits. We just didn't think he seemed all that smart, and so we figured we could solve his riddle. You need to get the answer for us. If not, we're going to take it out on you and your family" (Judges 14:15, paraphrased).

She goes back to Samson and asks him for the answer, but he won't tell. She says, "You don't really love me," and starts to cry. He says, "Fine, here's the answer: it's a lion and a bee." (Judges 14:16–17, paraphrased)

She tells her brothers, and they tell Samson. But Samson is so angry about this that he leaves the party, walks over to the next town, kills thirty Philistines, takes their fancy linen outfits, and brings them back to pay his debt (Judges 14:19). Then he leaves before the wedding even happens. This is not a stable individual we are dealing with here.

Sometime later, the text says, "at the time of wheat harvest" (Judges 15:1)—implying that an entire season has gone by—Samson decides he wants to see his "wife." But when he gets there, the family is like, "What are you talking about? You left months ago. She got married to some else" (Judges 15:2, paraphrased).

Samson now says to himself, "That's it, this time I am blameless. I have a right to get even" (Judges 15:3, paraphrased). He goes out, catches three hundred foxes, ties their tails together into 150 fox pairs, lights them on fire, and releases them into town (Judges 15:4–5). Everything gets burned up: the grain, the vineyards, the olive groves. He destroys everything. The men of the town blame this all on the woman and her family for bringing Samson into their lives, so they go and burn down the house with her and her father in it, killing them (Judges 15:6). Samson responds by viciously attacking and killing many of them in revenge (Judges 15:8).

The story is not done, though. The Philistines raise an army and prepare to attack Judah (Judges 15:9), but the leaders of Judah agree to hand Samson over in an effort to avoid a war (Judges 15:12). Except when they do, Samson breaks free, finds the jawbone of a donkey, and kills another thousand men. Then, just to rub it in, he writes a little poem to memorialize the day:

> *With a donkey's jawbone I have made donkeys of them.*
> *With a donkey's jawbone I have killed a thousand men.*

—*Judges 15:16*

Charming.

Now, this is an awful story. It's a long, sordid, embarrassing tale. It is not fit for children, and barely even for grown-ups, but it's what leads into the more familiar story of Samson that follows—the one with Delilah and the hair and the heroics. All of that seems to be part of a larger story demonstrating how God can redeem and use even the worst of us.

However, Samson sums up this first part of his story perfectly when he says, "I merely did to them what they did to me" (Judges 15:11). This probably isn't the verse most of us choose to define our lives, but it is certainly the verse that exemplifies exactly what revenge will do to any of us, eventually.

Samson tricks his neighbors with a riddle they can't solve. They trick him back by extorting the answer from his bride-to-be. Angry, he leaves before the marriage can happen. Hurt, she marries someone else. Frustrated, he burns down their fields. Enraged, they murder his estranged wife. Samson murders them back. The

Philistines raise an army to start a war. Samson finds a donkey bone and proceeds to go John Wick for the rest of the film, and in the end, a thousand people are dead over what amounts to a bad joke.

And yes, it's silly. It's supposed to be, because the story is about how absurd our revenge fantasies are and how they consume us if we let them. The point of the story is to walk you through this absurd tale and get you to the point where you read the words, "I only did to them what they did to me"—at which point, you realize that you have said the same thing before, somewhere along the line.

A desire for retribution is one of the most powerful emotions we experience as human beings. Think of the last movie you watched—I can almost guarantee there was some moment of comeuppance that made you smile.

John Wick killing the bad guys who killed his puppy.

"Hello. My name is Inigo Montoya. You killed my father. Prepare to die."[34]

Any time the protagonist is given permission to use "any means necessary."

Though these moments feel like justice to us, the problem, as Samson shows, is that it's always "justice plus one." You hurt me and so I inflict hurt back on you, plus one. Except now, not only are you hurt, but there's also a new perceived imbalance that needs to be rectified. The lex talionis is a containment strategy to rein this in.

MAKING PEACE

All of this is the context for Jesus' teaching on turning cheeks. "You have heard that it was said" (Matthew 5:38) is a reference to the lex talionis, and again, the law of retaliation is an ancient strategy we use to make sure revenge doesn't escalate uncontrollably. An eye for an eye was never designed to endorse violence. It was always about limiting the damage that revenge could cause. But along comes Jesus, who's not interested in just limiting damage, but who actually believes the damage can be undone, and says, "You've heard it said an eye for eye, and you've come to believe that this is the best we can do, but I tell you, there's something better."

And this is what Jesus thinks is better: if anyone slaps you on the right cheek, turn to them the left (Matthew 5:39). I'll admit, that doesn't sound much better, at first blush. Truth is, this often sounds like, and has been used to claim that, Jesus believes forgiveness means allowing some people to abuse you. That's a toxic idea, regardless of who it comes from.

However, there is a lot going on in the background of these images that dramatically influences how we hear them. One of the best treatments of this passage is by a scholar named Walter Wink. He talks about how, in the context of the ancient world, each of these specific examples Jesus cites is a clear act of social protest.

"If anyone slaps you on the right cheek, turn to them the other cheek also" (Matthew 5:39). In the ancient world, you always interacted with your right hand—the earthy details of which involve the fact that you would use your left hand to clean yourself after you used the ancient outhouse. In fact, one of the documents discovered in the Dead Sea Scrolls trove, a document called the Community Rule and designated 1QS, lays out a ten-day penance for gesticulating toward a community member with the left hand.[35]

Now, imagine yourself facing someone, and try to imagine that you were to strike that person using your right hand on their right check; that's a backhanded slap. In the world of Jesus, this was more than an assault—it was an attempt to assert social dominance. Backhanded slaps were used for humiliation and degradation. This is how a superior treated a subordinate. In the Roman world, this was how a master slapped a slave, a parent slapped a child, or a Roman slapped a Jewish person.

But now imagine if the person you intend to humiliate were to turn their right cheek away from you and their left cheek toward you. That would leave you with the option either to strike them with your left hand—undignified for you—or to strike them with an open hand—which, as strange as this is going to sound, offers dignity to them. A backhanded slap reminded the victim of their social status. An open-handed slap placed you in the same social strata as your assailant.

So, when Jesus says, "Turn to them your left cheek," he's not asking you to be slapped again. He's asking you to do something that will stop an abuser in their tracks, forcing them to see you in your essential dignity and humanity.

Next, Jesus says that if anyone takes your shirt, hand over your coat as well (Matthew 5:40). Now, "shirt" here is actually your underwear. The word is *chitona*,[36] which was actually the body-length piece of clothing that you would wear next to your skin. Coat is the word *himation*,[37] which was your main outer garment that you would wear around.

The context here is, no one would actually sue you for your underwear. That's silly, which is part of Jesus' point. You see, the Torah has specific rules forbidding the taking of someone's cloak. Exodus 22:8 says that if you take someone's cloak as a pledge, you have to return it to them by sunset, no matter what. That's because your cloak, or that outer garment, was what you would wear, what you would sleep in, what would keep you warm; it had all kinds of different uses in that world. So you can sue someone to take their house, or their livestock to repay their debts, but if all they have is their cloak, well, the Torah says that it is off limits.

Jesus is presenting this exaggerated scenario wherein someone is so consumed with revenge that they try to get around the rule, leaving your coat but suing you for your underwear. Remember Samson? Revenge can drive us to bizarre justifications. But in this absurd situation, if someone is that corrupted—if they want to diminish you that badly—then, in front of the world, you strip down, hand them everything, and let your refusal to be humiliated show everyone who the other person has become.

Finally, Jesus says, "If anyone forces you to go one mile, go with them two miles" (Matthew 5:41). "Going the extra mile" has entered our common vernacular as indicating a commitment to excellence, but the origins reach much deeper than that. Jesus' teaching here is rooted in the rules that governed the Roman army.

Jewish people were generally not Roman citizens. Though, like Paul, some were, most—including Jesus—were living in the Roman empire without the rights of a citizen. In Roman law, there was a clause about impressment that allowed a Roman soldier to conscript any non-citizen living under Roman protection to carry his bags for him for up to one thousand paces, or one Roman mile.[38] These types of impressment laws were common throughout human history in occupied lands, because they served both to subjugate the occupied population and also to ensure that military men did not overly abuse the populations (to the point of revolt).

Into this context, Jesus says that if someone tries to rob you of your autonomy simply because you are a non-citizen—if they treat you as less than human, or as a commodity to be used—then you remind them that your choices are yours. There is dignity in self-determination. Rome may be powerful, but you are still a living, breathing, thinking, human being who controls your own steps. In fact, continuing to carry a soldier's bags past a thousand paces puts that soldier in the awkward position of being in contravention of the rules his superiors handed down, so that he might even ask you to stop walking.

Jesus looks at the lex talionis and observes the way it limits the escalation of violence, but he sees that more is possible. He says, "You have heard it said that retribution is the best we can do, but I tell you, there is more. Do not use violence, but demand to be seen as an equal. Do not use violence, but demonstrate that you will not be humiliated by injustice. Do not use violence, but retain your autonomy in the face of subjugation."

In none of these examples is Jesus advocating for continued abuse or the idea that suffering itself leads to justice. He is advocating for specific, intentional, provocative actions designed to awaken the conscience of the world. Walter Wink writes that "human evolution has provided the species with two deeply instinctual responses to violence: fight or flight. Jesus offers us a third way: nonviolent direct action."[39]

Jesus is advocating for peacemaking in its most provocative sense, not simply the containment of our violence. Certainly, he is not endorsing continued suffering in exchange for the status quo. No, Jesus here invites us to participate in God's vision for the world—the creation of peace though confrontation with, and ultimately healing of, our violence.

But understand this, too: Jesus is not gaslighting you by asking you to subject yourself to abuse, to surrender your wellbeing to the courts, or to make friends with those who would oppress you. Jesus is inviting you to create peace in the world in a substantive way, by confronting injustice in terms that challenge the supremacy of violence in our world.

This is an extension of Jesus' point about abolishing or fulfilling the law. The law is the story that contains our worst instincts. It's like the curbs on the road that keeps us heading in the right direction. But to fulfill the law, to complete the intent behind the story, means we need to go beyond the law and create something new. An eye for an eye might prevent our revenge from spiraling out of control, but it will never make peace for anyone, and peacemaking is precisely what identifies us as part God's family.

PEACEMAKING THROUGH BOUNDARY-MAKING

Peacemaking, though, was always going to be much harder than violence prevention. As Jesus has already taught, it requires confronting injustice with nonviolent direct action. It requires us to refuse to play the game of violent one-upmanship but also to refuse to allow abuse to continue unhindered.

Yes, with much of his teaching, Jesus is speaking specifically to an oppressed group on the low end of the balance of power, but remember that there are a myriad of people and stories present for this particular sermon. Some of them are Roman, and though it's unlikely they are soldiers who have imposed impressment on those standing near them, they certainly benefit from the structural imbalances in Roman-occupied lands. Some of them are wealthy and powerful Jewish persons who assuredly have never sued anyone for their underwear but may have taken their less-wealthy neighbors to court. Some of them are masters, or parents, or husbands, who have used their social status to humiliate or degrade another human being.

And if we can't see all the ways that we ourselves are implicitly connected to these injustices, then perhaps we are not paying attention. White persons benefit from the fact that white culture is the water we swim in. Men benefit from the fact that patriarchy is still the unstated norm. Settlers benefit from stolen land that we now occupy and own by rule of law. Jesus' words are a call to provocative action when confronted with abuse, but they are no less a call to evaluate our actions and make changes when we are ones who have unwittingly perpetuated such abuse.

But, what happens when nonviolent direct action does not produce the intended result? Certainly, Jesus does not expect that every aggressive master, overzealous litigator, or lazy centurion will immediately recognize and repent of their actions when confronted. Further, what about when these imbalances happen closer to home, in personal relationships? How long can we safely turn the other cheek, knowing that such cheeky actions may exacerbate a volatile situation?

On that front, too, Jesus has wisdom for us. Remember always that the intent behind a law, oral or written, is more important than the letter. So if turning the other cheek no longer moves us toward that intent of peacemaking, we may need new creative expressions of the intent.

In Matthew's record of the sermon, Jesus adds, "You have heard that it was said, 'Love your neighbor and hate your enemy.' But I tell you, love your enemies and pray for those who persecute you" (Matthew 5:43–44). This already leans in the direction of the wisdom Jesus offers here, but we get perhaps a fuller picture of his intent by comparing this passage with the parallel in Luke. There, in an expanded account of this teaching, Jesus says, "Love your enemies, do good to those who hate you, bless those who curse you, pray for those who mistreat you'" (Luke 6:27–28). In fact, in Luke's account, this caveat actually precedes the instructions on cheeks and coats and miles. Now, perhaps you've read these words before but have never seen them characterized as a caveat, so let me explain.

Jesus opens this section by saying, in effect, "You've heard it said an eye for an eye, but I tell you, we can do better." Now he says, "You've heard it said, 'Hate your enemies,' but I tell you, that won't work, either." Instead, we can choose something different. And just as he offered three examples of nonviolent direct action, he offers alternatives to hating our enemies:

- Do good to those who hate you.
- Bless those who curse you.
- Pray for those who mistreat you.

It's really easy to blow past this, because it has the feel of something that a person like Jesus would say, but it's worth noting that this is actual poetry here. In the Hebrew culture, poetry often didn't rhyme, but it did heavily feature rhythm and wordplay. The central feature of Hebrew poetry is something we call parallelism, in which the poet states and then restates an idea, with increasing intensity or contrast each time. That's what Jesus is employing here, on two levels.

We've got someone who hates you, someone who curses you, and someone who mistreats you, and we've got the responses of doing good, blessing, and praying. With both injury and the response, each repetition in the triplet brings greater intensity. On the one side, you've got someone who has an intense, irrational dislike of you, which slowly eats at them until they begin to speak negatively about you, and which eventually consumes them as they begin to actively injure you. For some reason, the enmity in this relationship is spiraling out of control, and the lex talionis would function to ensure your responses remained in lock step.

Into this dilemma, Jesus proposes three things we can do: We can do good. We can speak well. We can hope for reconciliation. But there's a progression here as well, isn't there? Jesus says if someone hates you—maybe it's completely irrational, or perhaps you have done something to hurt them—you can go out of your way to show them who you really are. You can demonstrate your real character, or the way that you've changed, through concrete actions in the relationship. Where there are hard feelings, you can be there with a presence that offers healing and grace and models transformation as a possibility in that relationship. We take an active posture of pursuing reunion where it's possible.

Now, if they start to curse you—essentially, speaking bad things to you or about you—Jesus says you can do your best to speak well in return. Just as a slap does not receive a retaliatory slap, bad words don't require more bad words. I don't think Jesus intends for us to be untruthful. Any future reconciliation will always require an honest reckoning, so speaking truthfully is a must, but to bless is to choose the best true words. If their words are full of venom and bile, you can ensure that they are full of light and love. And that's harder than it sounds. Trust me. When someone is running you down, it's hard to lift them up, but Jesus' counsel is that when our first instinct is to return hurt with hurt, there is another option.

However, if that doesn't work—if nothing you do effects a change in that person, and they continue to spiral and escalate to mistreating you—then you can pray for them. Now, we have to pause here to acknowledge that mistreatment can absolutely be done with words. Abuse is far more than just broken bones, and I don't think that's the dividing line Jesus is making here. There is a point where someone has "only" cursed us, but there is a point where someone has gone too far. You need to feel that line for yourself.

But if they are mistreating you, Jesus says, you can pray for them. You do your best to heal yourself and forgive so that you can be free from them. There's a demarcation, though, that's happening in Jesus' advice here. When it's hate and hard feelings, you can be there in their life and work toward reunion. When it's bad words and gossip, you can take a step back but still choose not to descend into the mud with them. By contrast, when it has become abuse, mistreatment, and injury, you can heal and you can love that person from a distance, but you do not give that person access to yourself anymore. Let me be clear: you can forgive, you can love, you can pray, and you can honor the way of Jesus, and yet you absolutely can remove the person from your life. You can set up appropriate boundaries and healthy barriers to protect yourself, and you do this precisely so that you can choose to love your enemy and pray for them, and even forgive them whenever it is that you're ready to.

Jesus calls us to confront injustice with nonviolent direct action. He calls us to love our enemies, but he doesn't abandon us to abuse. As the intensity of the offence increases, so does your commitment to a better path, but this is going to necessitate an increase in your boundaries as well. Because you turn the other check, and hand over your cloak, and go the extra mile, you can do good, and speak well, and pray always, but loving your enemy is about creating peace in the world, not about allowing them to continue to hurt you. And part of our peacemaking in the world is demonstrating that while we choose love, we refuse to accept behavior that is damaging to the divine image in all of us.

In an interview with Russell Brand[40], Brene Brown talks about the importance of what she calls "boundaries of steel." She says the most compassionate people she has encountered are always the ones with the clearest and strongest boundaries. This seems very much in line with the depth and nuance behind Jesus' teaching here. To "turn the other cheek," we must have the clarity to name exactly what is wrong and the wisdom to determine the precise provocative action that will bring it to light. To "love our enemy," we must evaluate our injury honestly and determine the appropriate boundary that will stop the offence and leave open the possibility of transformation.

But hear me: you cannot love them by continuing to condone their actions. You cannot bless them by allowing them to steal the healing you need for yourself. You cannot pray for them unless you find a way to step back and create the boundaries that make your forgiveness possible, because healthy boundaries are not a sign of unforgiveness. They are the sign that you know what needs to be healed.

This is Jesus' call to us. To make peace—not by ignoring injustice, sweeping aside offence, or avoiding conflict, but by confronting what is wrong in the world and offering an alternative story. And in this story, the law that once contained our violence is completed in the actions that will one day put our violence to death.

WORKBOOK

Chapter Four Journal

Journal Prompt: In what situations have you encountered, or tried to exercise, the principle of "turning the other cheek"? In each context, to what extent did "turning the other cheek" reflect Jesus' approach of confronting injustice with nonviolent direct action? Think of specific ways you can make peace by establishing boundaries, in the sense Jesus taught, with those who hate, curse, or mistreat you personally.

_____

_____

_____

_____

_____

_____

_____

_____

_____

_____

_____

_____

CHAPTER FIVE

THE INTENT OF RIGHTEOUSNESS

OVER THE NEXT FEW chapters, we'll examine a section of this sermon often known as the Lord's Prayer, but we're going to focus on Jesus' approach to prayer rather than the specific prayer itself. As a precursor to this, it's worth exploring Jesus' teaching on righteousness—to help us better understand the relationship between action and prayer.

LEARNING TO RIDE

One summer, when my son was six years old, I wanted to get him on a bike. I ride a decent amount, and other than the fact that we live at the top of a relatively large hill, which means I have to ride up the incline to get home, a bike is a great way for us to traverse my city.

And my son likes my bike, too. We have one of those trailer bikes that attaches to my seat post, and he loves going for bike rides with that—mainly because he doesn't have to climb the hill to get to the top of the bluff near our house. He can just watch me drag him up the hill and laugh about how out of breath I am.

But that summer, we tried to get him on his own bike without training wheels, and we did not have a lot of success. It could have been due to my coaching; apparently, pointing him down a hill and yelling, "Pedal!" was not enough. Or it could have been how much easier it is when there's a perfectly good trailer bike right there and Dad can do all the work for you.

If you can remember back to when you learned to ride a bike, there's this weird moment when everything is awful and then, all of a sudden, it just sort of clicks. Someone has explained it, given you the instructions, sent you off down the hill by yourself, and watched you crash and fall over and over again. And every time, they just keep telling you the same thing: "Oh, it's easy—you just have to pedal." Well, obviously that's not helping, so maybe that's not *all* you have to do. And of course, it isn't all you have to do. You have pedal; you have to steer; you have to balance; you have to watch where you're going; you have to ensure your helmet is strapped on properly. There are thousands of calculations and corrections that you make constantly to ride a bike. It's incredibly complex, and yet, there is also a moment when all of it clicks.

And what happens is that all of this language, all of these rules, all of these instructions on how to ride a bike coalesce into an instinctive response whereby, all of a sudden, you're just doing it. Your momentum is carrying you, and you're not thinking about any of it anymore. This incredibly complex process, involving thousands of unconscious decisions, becomes shorthand for something so simple, you could never forget it: "it's like riding a bike."

Well, from everything history tells me, Jesus probably never learned to ride a bike, and yet, from the way he talks about the intersection of life and law and prayer, it seems to me that maybe he understands this process more intimately than we might expect.

PRACTISING RIGHTEOUSNESS

In Matthew chapter 6, Jesus says:

Be careful not to practice your righteousness in front of others to be seen by them. If you do, you will have no reward from your Father in heaven.

Wo, when you give to the needy, do not announce it with trumpets, as the hypocrites do in the synagogues and on the streets, to be honored by others. Truly I tell you, they have received their reward in full. But when you give to the needy, do not let your left hand know what your right hand is doing, so that your giving may be in secret. Then your Father, who sees what is done in secret, will reward you.

And when you pray, do not be like the hypocrites, for they love to pray standing in the synagogues and on the street corners to be seen by others. Truly I tell you, they have received their reward in full. But when you pray, go into your room, close the door and pray to your Father, who is unseen. Then your Father, who sees what is done in secret, will reward you. And when you pray, do not keep on babbling like pagans, for they think they will be heard because of their many words. Do not be like them, for your Father knows what you need before you ask him.

This, then, is how you should pray . . . .
—Matthew 6:1–9

Now, from that point, Jesus flows right into the Lord's Prayer. But first, let's look at this transition from law to prayer that Jesus walks us through in this section, because it's interesting to me that Jesus frames the law as having a deeper meaning, below the surface, beneath the words themselves, and that this is what leads him to prayer.

His message to us has been that the law is a story meant to shape us. But now he is telling us to be careful not to practice that story—of righteousness, justice, and law, which is all part of the same vocabulary for Jesus—in front of people. Part of the reason I find this so compelling is because, it seems to me, this is all part of the same argument for Jesus. Don't get caught up in the letter of the law, because the law isn't the point. Instead, the law is a pointer that moves you in the direction of the person you were meant to become.

If that's the case, and the law was always about changing you, then any attempt to use the law to enhance your social standing is always inherently missing the point. It's sort of like working hard to learn how to ride a bicycle but obsessing over how much you love the spandex shorts that come with it. If you listen through the surface of the examples Jesus uses, you can almost hear Jesus asking: "Are you interested in becoming the best version of yourself? Are you interested in allowing my story to slowly become your story? Are you interested in learning how to ride? Or are you merely interested in looking the part?"

Those are two very different concepts of righteousness. One is a righteousness where all of the lessons and skills come together so you can focus on the big picture of riding a bicycle well. And the other is a righteousness where you are so consumed with the minutiae of what an expert rider should or shouldn't do that you're unable to *be* an expert rider: pedal—steer—balance—look up—don't look down—keep your cadence—breathe in through your nostrils—scan for cars—stay in your lane—check your reflectors. The irony is that constantly trying to perform your righteousness leaves you with very little energy left to actually become the righteous person you want to be.

VIRTUE SIGNALING

In Jesus' day, this kind of public righteousness was defined by adherence to the Mosaic law. That's what Jesus is talking about here with his examples: commands to give alms to the poor, to fast, to pray—these are littered throughout the Hebrew Scriptures. And these would be some of the most visual and public displays of fidelity to the Torah you would see in that culture.

And to some extent, those markers still exist in our world in some fashion. Today, there are all kinds of niche communities within which we signal our righteousness to those around us. The term "virtue signaling" has become popular now, and often it gets levied against those who want to appear to be "woke." No doubt, there are those who want to appear progressive without doing the hard work of personal introspection. But the truth is that all across the political spectrum, from every perspective and position and posture, all of us are drawn toward signaling our intentions to those we want to impress. In fact, anyone who is castigating others for virtue signaling is in fact signaling their own virtue within their particular imagination of righteousness, aren't they? We all do it, all the time.

And to all of that, Jesus says, "If that's all you're interested in—signaling your righteousness to those who already agree with you, for a little bit of praise—well, then, congratulations, because it's yours." The secret Jesus has been driving toward from the very beginning is that whatever it is you want from your righteousness is what you will get out of it.

You can see this in how many times Jesus uses the word *reward* for both sides of his argument here: "they will have no reward," "they have received their reward," "your father will reward you . . . ." In fact, it's in there five times in this short section. The word *reward* is two different words in Greek, *misthos*[41] for the noun and *apodidōmi* for the verb.[42] But *reward* is the precise word for this in English, because it means the natural, normal consequence of your actions. It's not so much the gift; it's what's already coming to you, or what you deserve. In fact, both of these words can be used for your pay or your wage at work.

So, what Jesus means is that with God, your outcome is tied not to your performance but to your intent. If you want to signal your virtue and impress the people around you, if you want to be praised and looked up to, you'll probably get it, but that's the extent of it.

KNOWING OUR INTENT

Now, if what you truly want is to be transformed, if your intent is to find a new way of being, and if your hope is to discover the life within you—surrounding you, moving you along through the world with momentum—then that's exactly what you'll eventually find.

Generosity can get you praise, or generosity can free you from greed. Fasting can win you some fans, or fasting can remind you where your life comes from. Prayer can impress the people within earshot, or prayer can draw you into solidarity with those who surround you always. But all of it comes down to your intent.

And all of a sudden, I'm drawn back to the very beginning, the Beatitudes, where Jesus lays out his vision of the world and tells us how things could be. Where Jesus says, "Blessed are the pure in heart, for they will see God" (Matthew 5:8). It's not the well-performing or the highly praised; it's not those who get it right, or understand it, or put it all together in the right order. Purity here has nothing to do with our performance. It has everything to do with our heart and where we point it. I might even paraphrase Jesus this way: "Blessed are those who want nothing more than to discover the Divine, for they will see the truth of God."

If you want your praise, if you want admiration, if you want someone to look up to you and make you feel good about yourself—if that's what spirituality is for you—then fine, go for it. Just don't be disappointed when that's all you get out of it. But if you want to see God, if you want to discover life, if you want to stop overthinking and start enjoying the ride, if you want to be righteous because you want to connect to God and all the good that God breathed into the universe, then Jesus promises that this is what you will find on the other side.

For Jesus, our experience of religion is shaped not by how good we are at it, but by what we put into it. And when taken seriously, that is an incredibly freeing proposition, because it means we can finally stop judging ourselves and actually start living as we were meant to. This is why, when Jesus finally teaches us to pray—when he pulls all of this together and finally brings the law into conversation with the Divine—his model for prayer is characterized by the invitation to align our intentions with God.

WORKBOOK

Chapter Five Journal

Journal Prompt: Reflect on the idea that the law *is a pointer that moves you in the direction of the person you were meant to become.* Are you interested in becoming the best version of yourself? Are you interested in allowing Jesus' story to slowly become your story? Or are you merely interested in looking the part? Take an honest look at the intentions behind the "righteous" things you do and consider whether any of your intentions need realigning.

_____

_____

_____

_____

_____

_____

_____

_____

_____

_____

_____

_____

_____

CHAPTER SIX

ALIGNING OURSELVES WITH GOD

WHEN WE LEAVE CHURCH and go back to real life, and settle into real routines again, prayer can often feel confusing. After all—is prayer about worship? Is prayer about crossing our fingers and hoping for the best? Is prayer about snapping our fingers and telling God to get to work for us? Or is prayer all of that, or none of that, or more than that? Sometimes it feels like we're not supposed to talk about that confusion, and that makes it all that much harder to wrap our heads around the idea of prayer.

If you have ever struggled with prayer—how to do it, how to feel it, how to make sense of it—then I want you to know that we all struggle. I do, you do, and so did Jesus, friends. The fact that God is, and God cares, and God invites our story to be shared with God is always going to be a little overwhelming. But often, the pressure we feel to get prayer "right" has more to do with us than it does with God.

Edith Stein once said, "My longing for truth was a single prayer."[43] Meister Eckhart, one of my favorite Christian mystics, is often said—in several variations—to have opined, "If the only prayer you ever pray in your entire life is thank you then that will have been enough."[44]

Prayer really is where the rules don't matter and the points are made up. And yet, there are these tools, and these patterns, and there is wisdom handed down to us that can help us and shape us as we go, and that's what Jesus invites us to consider. However, please remember that at the end of the day, I think any honest expression of wonder pointed toward the Divine counts as sacred prayer.

IMITATING THE MASTERS

In this last chapter, we likened the idea of living a righteous life to learning to ride a bike. Now I'd like to use the analogy of learning to play the guitar for learning how to pray. I play the guitar—not very well, but I do have the hair for it at least. However, when you're starting out, one of the first things you do is learn your scales. And what you're doing is learning which notes to include and which ones to leave out when you play.

Somewhat ironically, being limited to certain notes helps you become more creative with them. In Christianity, this is what we call liturgy. Liturgy is when we are given prayers like the Lord's Prayer as a guide or a model, which can sometimes feel restricting at first, as if our opportunity for self-expression is being limited. But really, what happens is that once we learn the scale, and see what Jesus is doing—once we internalize his patterns—what we find is this infinite space where our hopes and fears, and our frustrations and joy, are welcomed into the presence of God. We're learning the scales so that we can then play the music of prayer.

And when we learn to play guitar, we're learning to imitate the masters. You pick up a guitar because you want to learn how to play like your musician idols. For most of us, as teenagers, that meant long hours standing in front of a mirror, holding a guitar and practising how to look like a rock star, more than anything else. But sometimes, you also practice the music, and over time that repetition and that imitation build your skills. There comes a time when we fall back on that imitation and the familiarity of old patterns, but imitation leads to innovation.

So, you learn those guitar parts inside out, and like riding a bike, you never forget them. This really is a lot of what prayer looks like in the Bible. It is creative and free and unique and beautiful, but it's also somehow an imitation of someone else. Even Jesus, in his most vulnerable moment, falls back on the words of someone else to express himself (Matthew 27:46, cf. Psalm 22:1), and this is beautiful.

We don't always need to know what to say, and in fact, sometimes it's better not to know what to say for ourselves and instead allow someone else to speak for us in that moment. This is holy, because it is in itself an act of surrender. One of the most meaningful ways that I have made peace with prayer in my life is coming to realize that it's not always about me. When I stop trying to be creative, stop trying to be eloquent, and stop trying to express myself, what I often find is a freedom to simply be in the presence of the one I've been looking for. When I stop trying to make it happen, and I simply surrender to the prayers I have received, oftentimes, I find that it was my efforts that were getting in the way of noticing God is with me. Part of prayer is allowing the prayers of others to speak for us.

A DEEPER LOOK AT THE LORD'S PRAYER

Thankfully, Jesus offers us a prayer we can receive and imitate:

> *Our Father, who art in heaven,*
> *hallowed be thy name;*
> *thy kingdom come;*
> *thy will be done;*
> *on earth as it is in heaven.*
> *Give us this day our daily bread.*
> *And forgive us our trespasses,*
> *as we forgive those*
> *who trespass against us.*
> *And lead us not into temptation;*

but deliver us from evil.
For thine is the kingdom,
the power and the glory,
for ever and ever.
Amen.

Now we're going to look at this prayer, the Lord's Prayer, and see what we can pull from it in order to better understand prayer in our own lives. But before we dive in, we have to go back to a key point from the last chapter: when Jesus teaches about prayer, he does so in the context of a conversation about righteousness.

The word we translate as *righteousness* is translated as *justice* in Greek and Hebrew and French and Spanish, and many other languages except for English.[45] So, when we talk about righteousness, we need to remember that we are speaking about pursuing a more just world. In fact, in Greek, the word used in Matthew is *dikiaosune*, the primary meaning of which is "the quality, state, or practice of judicial responsibility, with focus on fairness, justice, equitableness, fairness . . . ."[46] Further, when Jesus turns to discussing and demonstrating prayer for his disciples in Matthew 6:5–15, what has he just been talking about? Justice for the poor (Matthew 6:1–4). So these are the ideas floating around in Jesus' mind when he turns his attention to prayer: responsibility, fairness, equitableness, and justice.

Prayer is a subset of our practice of righteousness, and righteousness is our participation with justice in the world. We're not talking about following the rules and not speeding and paying for your parking, although all of that is good. We're talking about working alongside God for a more just, equitable, fair world, or in Jesus' words—a kingdom on earth like God's above. That's what the prayer of Jesus is predicated on, and so, it's what we have to keep firmly in our minds as we begin to study this prayer. We must remember that this prayer, and all prayer, is designed to help us become better participants in God's world, not merely more religious ones.

GOD AS OUR FATHER

Now, if you turn to Matthew chapter 6, you're going to see the Lord's Prayer starting in verse 9, but it's not going to look exactly like what we read a moment ago. The prayer ends in verse 13 with, "and lead us not into temptation, but deliver us from the evil one," period. And then, from there, Jesus goes on talking, but most of us are used to praying, "For thine is the kingdom, the power and the glory, forever and ever. Amen."

That benediction actually did show up in early manuscripts of Matthew from around the fifth century. We call these the Majority Texts, or the Byzantine Texts; they are most common texts we have. These are what the King James was translated from, in the 1600s, which is where that benediction originated. So those lines are very old, at least 1,500 years old. But they're not there in the earliest fragments of Matthew, which come from the city of Alexandria in about the second century.[47]

So, what likely happened is that either a scribe came along and realized that this prayer had been given to the church, and wanted it to be used in worship, so he wrote a nice little flourish that helped tie it together with a bow.[48] Or perhaps he realized that it already was being used in worship and people were already saying it with this addendum, so he decide to add it into the text for us.

This shows us just how organic the original collection and dissemination of the Scriptures were in the early church, but it also shows the painstaking work that's done by scholars to try to recreate these texts for us as they originally were written by their authors.

So while you will still read the benediction in your King James Bible, modern translations have generally omitted the lines that were not part of Jesus' original words. You won't find the benediction in the New International Version (NIV) or the English Standard Version (ESV), for example, but in worship, we generally include it when we recite the prayer as part of the work of the church. And as a side note, I actually find it quite a beautiful expression, almost a metaphor, for this partnership between heaven and earth into which Jesus is absolutely, unapologetically going to invite us through this prayer.

Right from the start of this prayer, Jesus is taking us somewhere: "Our Father in heaven, hallowed be your name" (Matthew 6:9). Immediately, I notice that Jesus starts his prayers differently than I do. I recognize, at some level prayer is conversation, in which I am generally in the habit of addressing my audience, perhaps something like, "Gracious God," "Heavenly Father," or "Jesus"—these are all ways that I tend to start a prayer. At times I will string them together, "Almighty God, gracious God, loving God." These are all attributes that I want to centre myself in as I approach the Divine in prayer.

I think it's normal and healthy that we choose to remind ourselves whom we're speaking to, in prayer. Sometimes, simply remembering that God is good, that God is gracious, that God is loving, and that God is on your side, before you begin, can transform your experience of the conversation that follows.

And yet, I can't help but notice that Jesus centres himself in something very different as he begins to pray. Now, it's no less gracious, no less loving, but it is significant. Commentators have picked up on this for thousands of years. In fact, many traditions have taken to calling this prayer the "Our Father" for this very reason. The attributes of God that Jesus wants to centre himself in—are God's "father-ness" and God's "our-ness."

Greek is a funny language for an English speaker to make sense of, in part because the order of words functions differently than we are used to. In Greek, you can basically put the words together in whatever order you want, in order to emphasize or diminish something. In Greek, this prayer begins *Pater* (father) *hēmōn* (first plural genitive pronoun), or literally, "father of us." So, father is actually the first word. Some people get caught up on that "father" bit. Either people want to plant some kind of flag in a masculine identity for the Divine or they want to push back against that. Personally, I think both responses have the potential to miss Jesus' point here. The Divine simply transcends simple binaries.

What Jesus is doing is not attempting to ground God in the masculine so much as ground the Divine in the experience of a chosen family. And absolutely, it's a metaphor that was culturally appropriate to its context, but it is also a metaphor that speaks to something true—that God is not distant, that God is close and tender and loving as a parent should be, no matter when or where you begin that relationship.

I understand that it's possible your experience of a parent, of a father or a mother, was not all that it should have been, and it's possible that for you, those words do not convey the meaning they were intended to, but the beauty in this image is the chosen-ness of the language. We are invited to choose God as parent because God has chosen us as children. This is not an autocratic God saying, "Call me Dad from now on"; this is an invitation to create new meaning within the concept of family as it comes to us, regardless of the words we choose to use.

The word *pater* that's used here probably points us back to the Aramaic *abba*, which means something like "Dad," but for the record, *abba* is more like Dad than Daddy. *Abba* is the familiar, loving word for Father in Aramaic; it's not an infantilizing word.[49] So to talk about God as Father or *pater* or *abba* or Dad isn't about taking away our agency or making us small—it's about allowing ourselves to sink into everything that family could be, made holy.

When I pray, what this reminds me of, what this centres me in, is my complete safety in that momentthat I have no one to impress, no one to persuade, no one who needs to know just how smart or eloquent or convincing I can be, because I am, in that moment, actually, already, fully and completely known.

HEAVEN IS HERE

Our Father in heaven is actually our father in the heavens. This is intriguing because in the next line, Jesus says, "Your kingdom come, your will be done, on earth as it is in heaven" (Matthew 6:10), singular.

So, what's going on here? Well, *the heavens* are a lot more fluid in Greek. The word is *ouranos,* or in the plural *ouranois,*[50] but you have to remember that in Hebrew thought, heaven was not some distant place in the clouds to which we all aspire; it was more like a way of talking about what could be, or maybe what should be, in the world.[51] So heaven was where God was, but heaven was also *wherever* God was.

Ouranos was also used for "the skies," and this is why we often think of "heaven above." But that also included everything from the stars at night, to the clouds above, to the air that you breathe. In fact, later in this same sermon, in verse 26, Jesus is going to talk about worry, and he's going to say, "Look at the birds of the air; they do not sow or reap or store away in barns, and yet your heavenly Father feeds them. Are you not much more valuable than they? Can any one of you by worrying add a single hour to your life?" Well, when he talks about the birds of the "air" and your "heavenly" father, he's using the same word, *ouranos,* in the same sentence, to talk about both.

So heaven is large. It's the metaphorical concept of God's reigning and ruling; it's the stars in the sky and the clouds above you; it's the world reunited with the Divine. It is the air that birds glide through and the breath that fills your lungs. All of this is the heaven God occupies. And I wonder if the reason Jesus uses the plural here is to say that even now, God is present in every expression of the heavens—that God is there, ahead of us, in everything that we hope for, but also here in the air that we breathe right now. In fact, I don't think this is just a literary quirk. I think Jesus is trying to root our imagination of the Divine at the intersection of heaven and earth, as if maybe that spiritual/physical boundary we hold in our minds is not as indicative of reality as we imagine. That maybe God moves more freely though our lives than we have allowed for.

If you have ever imagined God as up and away and distant from you, out there somewhere, then perhaps as you pray, you might remember that the heavens are as close as the air you breathe, literally, and that God is present in all of it right now.

Jesus says, "Your kingdom come, your will be done, on earth as it is in heaven" (Matthew 6:10). Prayer is, at its heart, about hope—believing that the earth is salvageable, that the earth is redeemable and that we have a part to play in that story of repair. However, I find it helpful here to translate this section as literally as possible to really hear what Jesus is saying. This phrasing is going to sound awkward, but it might be helpful to hear what Jesus says at its most raw: "Come kingdom of you, be born desire of you, as in heaven, now also on earth."

For me, this is incredibly helpful because I find it very easy to pray, "Your kingdom come, your will be done on earth as it is in heaven," and to imagine this as some kind of cosmic conquest, like God is going to give us freedom whether we want it or not, guiding us, almost forcing us into paradise, if you will.

But to pray it more literally changes how I experience the prayer. Notice the use of the word *born*—the Greek verb *ginomai,* which means, "to come into being through process of birth or natural production, *be born.*"[52] To know it's not just that God's will is being done, but that God's will is being born, created, and formed within the world, within me, makes for a very different experience of prayer. No longer am I asking God to do anything. Instead, I'm asking myself to align with what God is already doing all around me.

I wonder if this is what Jesus was getting at when just before his prayer, he says that God already knows what you need before you ask, so don't go on about it. For a long time, I always wondered, if God knows, why ask? If God understands, why tell? If God is always there, then why bother speaking at all? I mean, why not just learn to rely on the omnipotence of the Divine and call that prayer?

But what I've come to realize is that the asking, and the telling, and the speaking of prayer were never for God, anyway; they were always for me. Nowhere else in my life do I get to ask without explaining, and very rarely in my life do I get to tell my story without wanting to position myself in some advantageous way. Nowhere else do I speak without fear of miscommunication or misunderstanding of meaning. But here, in prayer, with my chosen family in God, the irony of knowing that God already knows means that none of that work that I normally do to protect myself holds any meaning anymore.

And sure, I do still try. I try to sell God on my ideas, and I try to position myself in the best light possible as I pray. I still try to make sure that my words carry my intent with clarity, but in those moments where I know God as father, and see God as mother, and experience God as pure love beyond limitation, I know that what I hide behind doesn't matter anymore. Here in prayer, I know that if I don't have the words, I can plagiarize someone else. I know that if my "ask" is insane, I can go for it anyway.

Because I know that if I'm wrong—I am loved.

If I'm ashamed—I am welcome.

If I'm confused—I am comforted.

If I'm lying—I am listened to.

If I'm honest—I am taken seriously.

If I'm funny—I can expect divine laughter.

If I am crying—God will never tell me to be a man.

Because prayer is where I am nothing but who I am, and I am embraced like a beloved child, regardless.

So, when we begin our prayers with, "Our father who art in heaven," the intent here is not to remind us of the masculinity of God or the distance to the Divine, but instead to ground ourselves in the overwhelming experience of beloved family, because from Jesus' perspective, God is for us.

And it's a really big deal that in prayer, I remember that God is not mine. God is not *my* father. God is not *my* Saviour, my own personal Jesus who lives in *my* heart. The Divine is fundamentally *ours*. I know this might seem like I'm making too big a deal out of one pronoun here, but honestly, without exaggeration, how we remember *our* here will reshape everything about how we pray.

Is prayer an expression of some unique and special connection I have with *my* God, or is prayer an expression of some fundamental human connection with the Divine shared by everyone who breathes? Because if it's the former, then I can go on with my day the way I started, with a focus on me, but if it is the latter, if prayer is about my connection both to God and to you, then I am brought squarely back to the justice that Jesus tells us is our starting point for prayer.

JUSTICE IS THE POINT OF PRAYER

Jesus grounds prayer in two essential ideas: first, that God is near to us and invested in what is good for us personally, and second, that God is near to all of us and invested in what is good for every one of us collectively.

And that includes the "everyones" we struggle with, too. After all, when Jesus says not too pray like the hypocrites who look for attention, but instead to pray like this, "Our Father," he is explicitly calling us to include even those hypocrites we encounter in our "our."

Now, I know you pray for those hypocrites, and I know you pray for your enemies, because I pray all kinds of things for those who I wish would do things differently, but things change for me when I learn to pray *with* the hypocrites and *beside* my enemies. Elbow to elbow in prayer with those who see God differently than I do every time I start with "our." In fact, I would argue that Jesus calls me to include in my "our" those whose "our" does not include me, and that's often really hard.

Way back in the beginning, in Genesis, there is this story about the archetypal first family, with a man named Adam, and his name means "dirt" or "soil."[53] There's also a woman, called Eve, whose name means "life" or "life-giving."[54] And Dirt and Life come together and have children, including a son named Abel, which means "breath,"[55] and another named Cain, which means "acquire."[56]

And one day, Acquire, who is very concerned about who gets the most praise, kills his brother Breath out in a field. Breath's blood cries out to God, and God goes to see Acquire and asks, "What has happened to your Breath?" But Acquire says, "I don't know anything about Breath. Am I my brother's keeper?"

In many ways, everything that follows as you read your Bible is God saying yes to that question. Of course you are your brother's keeper. Of course your neighbor is your responsibility. Of course you are meant to live out of your essential connectedness to every other living (Alive) person on the earth (Dirt). So God tells stories, and God makes rules, and God forgives, and God mourns, until finally Jesus comes along and says, "Listen, if you want to know God, then this is how you should pray." And this prayer starts with "our"—with acknowledging your essential connectedness to everyone.

Ron Rolheiser writes:[57]

> Our Father . . . who always stands with the weak, the powerless, the poor, the abandoned, the sick, the aged, the very young, the unborn, and those who, by victim of circumstance, bear the heat of the day. . . . Who art in heaven . . . where everything will be reversed, where the first will be last and the last will be first, but where all will be well and every manner of being will be well. Hallowed be that name . . . .

Prayer is properly an expression of intimacy directed up toward God only insofar as it engenders an expression of intimacy that extends horizontally, to those around us as well. God extends intimacy to us; we extend love to those around us. And that kind of prayer is how you get your breath back even if you have spent too much time focusing on yourself.

To pray the "Our Father" is to pray in solidarity with all those who know God and those who don't, trusting that the story of Genesis and our dissolution into "us and them" can all be reversed. It might be hard at times to believe that God is your Father, but trust me, it is a much bigger thing to believe that God is *our* Father. Because when you say, "Our Father," that means that you are now, by extension, your brother's keeper: your Muslim sister's keeper, your homeless brother's keeper, your co-working sibling's keeper, and your Christian neighbor's keeper—all of that, in the exact same breath.

So this is what we do when we pray: We remind ourselves of who we are when we pray. We remind ourselves of who God is when we pray. And we align ourselves with that imagination as we pray. All that we might be like God, and that earth might be like heaven. Prayer is not where God decides what will happen to us, but instead where we decide who we will become as we pursue God out of our prayers and back into the world.

So pray well. Remember God as intimate and tender, and come to know that space free from performance or compulsion. May you experience God as fully "ours," completely present to you and to those near you, and through it all, may you then choose to be like God, to become your brother's keeper and your neighbor's support and your stranger's best friend. May you work to dispel the illusion that we are on our own sometimes, and may your narrow slice of the earth become a little more like heaven as you do.

WORKBOOK

Chapter Six Journal

Journal Prompt: Reflect on the explanation of the phrase *"Our* Father" in this chapter. *You see, prayer is properly an expression of intimacy directed up toward God only insofar as it engenders an expression of intimacy that extends horizontally as well, to those around us, as God extends intimacy to those around us.* Write out a prayer modeled after this element of prayer.

_____

_____

_____

_____

_____

_____

_____

_____

_____

_____

_____

_____

_____

CHAPTER SEVEN

Resting in God's Goodness

I said earlier that prayer is not for God, but for me, and that is undoubtedly true. Sometimes, though, I also think prayer is *to* me. Now, not that I pray to myself—even for someone with an ego, that's a bit much—but I do recognize that prayer is sometimes, maybe often, about speaking truth to myself. God is my audience, but often my words are truly intended for my own heart.

When I pray, "Come your kingdom, be born your desire, as in heaven, now in me," who are those words intended for, if not me? This is prayer as sacred self-talk. I know that when I say that, you may feel like I am diminishing prayer, but believe me, I am not. We know just how important self-talk is for us as human beings—that we create narratives in our minds and we construct our reality as we describe our world for ourselves. But prayer has always been, for thousands of years, where we are invited to understand the best version of ourselves in front of the one who fashioned us.

If there is anyone who is ever going to believe the best about you, it's the one who put everything good in you to begin with. Prayer is where we come to believe that we are the person God believes we are. When you pray, part of prayer is asking how the best version of you can help to close the gap between heaven and earth today. This is how prayer helps to shape your story and the stories around you in new ways.

But Jesus is not done, not even close, and so even as he invites us to engage in sacred self-talk, Jesus calls us to trust in something beyond ourselves as well.

DAILY BREAD

"Give us today our daily bread." This is an interesting line because of the somewhat curious repetition: "Give us *today* our *daily* bread." Jesus is notoriously pithy; he likes to say what he thinks in short, memorable ways, and in my experience, Jesus doesn't speak carelessly, so the repetition here is probably noteworthy.

What makes it complicated is the word that's translated as *daily bread*—the Greek *epiousios*[58]—because we don't really know exactly what that means. It doesn't show up anywhere, in that construction, except here. However, we do understand that it is a compound word made from *epi* and *ousia*,[59] and depending on how you put those together, you're going to come up either with what's necessary for today or with what's needed for tomorrow.

So even though "give us today our daily bread" is pretty firmly entrenched in our religious vocabulary, most scholars today tend toward interpreting this phrase as "give us today our bread for tomorrow." And that's significant because it is a callback to a story from Exodus 16. The people of God are stuck wandering in the wilderness, and they think they will starve, but God sends miraculous bread for them to eat. It's called manna, which in Hebrew translates—I'm not kidding—to something like, "what should we call this stuff?" (Exodus 16:15, paraphrase). Personally, I think it's awesome that such a delightfully unpretentious term stuck.

This miracle manna bread would appear in the morning, and the Israelites could gather it and use it and eat it all day. But if they tried to gather more than they needed, and stockpile it, it would rot overnight and be inedible by the morning (Exodus 16:19–20). The whole story is about learning to trust God for what they needed, not their ability to store and hoard for the future.

That's almost certainly what Jesus is getting at here. Prayer is about our learning to be continually dependent on God. Prayer is not about turning to God when you have a problem; prayer is, at its best, a continual awareness of dependence and need. It's knowing that need is your normal, natural state, and it always has been—and that's hard. For most of us, everything we have been taught to believe about ourselves, everything we have been trained to work toward in our lives, has been about independence and self-sufficiency, rugged individualism and bootstrapped competency.

But Jesus says that's not even close. It's God who causes the rain to fall on the just and the unjust, and you may have worked hard, but everything you have is ultimately a gift. Prayer is where you remember that.

I don't think for a second this precludes turning to God when you have a specific need; in fact, I think it invites it, because if we know that today is gift—that this meal is a gift, and this moment is a gift—then we realize that everything is a dance of gift and reception, whether we know to ask or not. But, when we learn to pray for the mundane, then everything becomes available to us in prayer, and maybe that's the point.

At the same time, there's something strange in what Jesus prays, because if this is a callback to Exodus, and if we are meant to remember the story of the manna, it's kind of odd that Jesus would pray, "Give us today our bread for tomorrow." After all, the whole point of the story of the manna was not to store bread for tomorrow, right?

Well, the exception was the Sabbath. On the day before the Sabbath, the Israelites were instructed to gather two days' worth of food and to use that while they rested and worshiped God. And somehow, on that day, once a week, the food would last an extra day.

Maybe the point that Jesus is intimating here, by talking about being given today our bread for tomorrow, is that prayer is where we learn to rest—that is, prayer is a gift, because prayer is also Sabbath. It's important to realize that prayer is not work; prayer is not gathering. It's not asking, and it's not making your case before God. Prayer is simply learning to rest in the goodness of God.

Please understand that I don't say this flippantly or lightly. I don't mean that everything will be okay because you prayed. I mean that God is good and that sometimes the best we can do is rest in that, because prayer is about learning to trust in just enough. And for a lot of us who are used to more than just enough, this might be the hardest thing that Jesus faces us with, in this prayer.

FORGIVE AS YOU HAVE BEEN FORGIVEN

Jesus prays, "Forgive us our debts ["trespasses," in the King James], as we also have forgiven our debtors ["those who trespass against us," in the King James]." This is not an uncommon idea, for Jesus to link forgiveness with forgiveness. Immediately after the Lord's Prayer, Jesus clarifies what he meant, saying in verses 14 to 15, "For if you forgive other people when they sin against you, your heavenly Father will also forgive you. But if you do not forgive others their sins, your Father will not forgive your sins."

That is a heavy thought—to know that forgiveness is linked inextricably with forgiveness. Analyzing Jesus' words can get kind of technical, but breaking them down doesn't really do anything to take away their sting. Jesus prays, "Forgive us our debts as we also have forgiven our debtors." That little word *as* is the word *hos* in Greek, and it opens up some room in the relationship between the two clauses. The question comes down to whether the relationship is temporal or interdependent.

In English, this is usually translated: Forgive us (present tense), as we have forgiven others (past tense). That makes one a condition of other, as if it's a temporal relationship: "God, forgive us after we forgive others." What complicates this is that in the manuscripts, the second appearance of *forgive* is often spelt wrong, so in most of the manuscripts, it looks like it's in the present tense—or at least, it's closest to that spelling. However, some scholars think that the way it's misspelt is indicative of something else—that it was intended to be in aorist tense, which would be closer to our past tense in English. And because the conjunction *hos* that links them can work either way, we don't really have a definitive answer, at least not based on this one particular verse. Welcome to the joys of textual criticism.

But what happens is that what you are left with is either, "God, forgive us after we have forgiven," or "God, forgive us in the way that we are forgiving, or at least learning to forgive." Neither way removes the sting, because either way, this is a hard teaching, but it does present some interesting questions.

When we take into account everything that Jesus says and does and demonstrates in his life, it seems to me that the second option is preferable here. Forgiveness is not something you buy; it's not something you either earn or you don't. It's something you learn to live in. I think the reason you can only be forgiven as much as you learn to forgive is not because God holds anything against you—you are always loved—but because, until you learn to let go of the past, you're always holding on to it. If you're holding on to an old offence, you're putting up barriers to experiencing forgiveness yourself, because you're refusing to live here, now, at the present, wherein forgiveness is.

This is why repentance and forgiveness are so central to the Christian story: because as long as you carry the hurt, the wound, the sin, and the brokenness with you, and you refuse to put it down, you will never know the welcome, the embrace, and the freedom that God desperately wants you to experience. We pray not to change God's mind about us—God never changes—but rather, we pray so we can let go of everything that stops us from seeing ourselves as God sees us today. And this is how God leads us to a better tomorrow.

GOD DOES NOT TEMPT US

Jesus prays, "Lead us not into temptation, but deliver us from evil." Again, I'll grant, this is sort of an odd saying. I mean, why would God be leading us into temptation in the first place? If God is always forgiving, and desperately wants us to know ourselves as forgiven, then why, God, are you trying to trip us up now, at the end of the prayer?

This, too, is sort of a quirk of translation. Pope Francis made some news when he was quoted talking about the need to update the Lord's Prayer, and he was praising the decision by the bishops in France to adjust the prayer in French. He said:[60]

> This is a translation that's not good. Even the French have changed the text, to a translation that says: "Don't let me fall into temptation," that I'm the one who falls. But it's not Him who throws me into temptation, in order to then see how I've fallen. No, a father doesn't do this. A father helps you to get up right away. The one who leads us into temptation is Satan

Regardless of what you think about this as a matter of translation, the Holy Father is on very solid ground here as far as interpreting Jesus' words. James 1:13 says, "Let no one say when they are tempted, 'I am tempted by God', for God cannot tempt with evil. God tempts no one; each person is tempted when they are lured and enticed by their own desires."

And on the matter of translation, I will quote from the Catechism of the Catholic Church, paragraph 2,846, which says:[61]

> This petition goes to the root of the preceding one, for our sins result from our consenting to temptation; we therefore ask our Father not to "lead" us into temptation. It is difficult to translate the Greek verb used by a single English word: the Greek means both "do not allow us to enter into temptation" and "do not let us yield to temptation.

Bottom line, God does not tempt us with evil; on the contrary, God wants to set us free, so we ask God not to stand by as we take the way that leads to sin. The point here is, prayer is where we are learning to say no to what hurts us so that we can follow the ways that God is actually leading us.

Understand, God is not leading you somewhere to trick you. God is not trying to trip you or test you. God is not trying to stretch you or catch you in a moment of weakness to show you how terrible you are, and if that's the imagination of the Divine that has been handed to you, it does not come from God, because God is ahead and behind, and above and around; God is in and through every step you take—when you notice it, and when you don't. So God is never that voice calling you toward what hurts you. God is the one who invites you into everything that will make you whole, and that's what Jesus grounds us in, through his prayer.

This is what Jesus prays, in effect: "Our Father in the heavens, help me to live in light of the truth that you are the source of all that is good in the universe. May your will be born in me so that I might help close the gap between heaven and earth with my choices. Remind me of my daily dependence on you and help me to want for just enough. Teach where I need to let go of old hurts so that I can experience forgiveness fully for myself. And show me where I need to say no so that I can truly follow the path that leads to life. For thine is the kingdom, the power, and glory, forever and ever, amen."

And maybe that prayer is helpful for you. Maybe the same ideas with slightly new language will open you to the goodness of God all over again. And maybe, as you read it, and metabolize it, you will begin to pray it, first in these words and then in your own. After all, the more we imitate, the more room for creativity we slowly uncover. Eventually, you may find Jesus' words become your words in new ways.

WORKBOOK

Chapter Seven Journal

Journal Prompt: Reflect on the explanation of forgiveness in this chapter: *As long as you carry the hurt, the wound, the sin, and the brokenness with you, and you refuse to put it down, then you will never know the welcome, the embrace, and the freedom that God desperately wants you to experience.* Meditate on the idea that perhaps the depth of your understanding of how much you've been forgiven affects your capacity to forgive others. Ask for a deeper understanding of how fully you are forgiven and how that forgiveness should fully extend to other people.

_____

_____

_____

_____

_____

_____

_____

_____

_____

_____

_____

_____

CHAPTER EIGHT

GOD'S IDEA OF THE GOOD LIFE

THERE IS A PROBLEM when we speak of the pursuit of happiness: everyone has a different measure for what will make them happy. That's why real conversations about wealth and satisfaction and happiness have to reach behind the figures and into our perceptions of the world.

In fact, there's good research that shows wealth does make you happy, up to a certain point. But money doesn't actually go as far in this regard as we sometimes assume it does. Money can provide you access to the basics and a little bit more, and the basics do make you happy up to a point, but beyond that basic level of income—which is not insubstantial, especially in certain places—there doesn't seem to be much to your happiness except your perception.

In his book, *The Paradox of Choice: Why More Is Less*, psychologist Barry Schwartz argues that having too many options actually impairs our happiness.[62] He argues that the human psyche is paralyzed by a preponderance of choice. We call this F.O.M.O., fear of missing out.

Certainly, there's a point where wealth gives you access to what you want, and that's good and healthy and makes you happy. But then wealth hits a tipping point, where it gives you access to more than you can handle, and it starts to work against you. When I can afford a good thing, that's great, but when I can afford ten good things yet only have the time and energy to choose one of them, it's stressful. What happens, according to happiness researchers, is that a lot of the energy we would normally invest in enjoying that good thing gets expended deciding on what good thing to enjoy—which diminishes our enjoyment, which in turn makes us think we chose poorly, which makes us anxious about the other options we're missing out on because we didn't choose them.

Now look, I'm not telling you to feel bad for wealthy people, but what I'm saying is that the relationship between wealth and happiness is not the straight line we imagine. And this is why the ancients talked not about the pursuit of happiness, but instead about the good life. This idea was based on a Greek word, *eudaimonia*, that often gets translated as "happiness," but is probably something more like "blessing," or "flourishing," or simply the good life.[63]

There were all kinds of attempts to explain the good life throughout philosophical history. Plato and Aristotle thought it was tied up in virtue. The Epicureans thought it was bound to hedonism: that sort of "eat, drink, and be merry, for tomorrow we die" kind of attitude. The Stoics thought it was all about ethics and knowing how to act in any situation. But one of the things all these philosophical schools seemed to understand was that happiness or flourishing, eudaemonia, was far more than our external circumstances. Those matter, of course, but real happiness was always rooted somewhere deeper, which is also what Jesus seems to be talking about in this passage we will explore next.

MAMMON: THE WORSHIP OF WEALTH

In Matthew 6:19–24, Jesus says:

> *Do not store up for yourselves treasures on earth, where moths and vermin destroy, and where thieves break in and steal. But store up for yourselves treasures in heaven, where*

*moths and vermin do not destroy, and where thieves do
not break in and steal. For where your treasure is, there
your heart will be also.*

*The eye is the lamp of the body. If your eyes are
healthy, your whole body will be full of light. But if your
eyes are unhealthy, your whole body will be full of darkness. If then the light within you is darkness, how great is
that darkness!*

*No one can serve two masters. Either you will hate
the one and love the other, or you will be devoted to the
one and despise the other. You cannot serve both God and
money.*

This is interesting because, I think, Jesus is actually saying
the same thing three times in this passage: store up treasures in
heaven; the eye is the lamp of the body; you can't serve two masters. All of these are about how wealth can distract us from what is
really good and meant for our flourishing.

I'm going to pick on the NIV translation here for a moment,
because as much as I do appreciate this version, they've made an
interesting choice in this instance with the word *vermin*. What they
are talking here about are rats, and that's certainly part of what Jesus
has in mind, but he doesn't literally say "rats." The word he uses is
brosis, which is the Greek word for the act of consumption.[64] And
given that he is talking about the act of consumption and moths,
it's pretty reasonable to assume that he means vermin—which he
does, in a sense. Rats would be one of the most common, if not
the most common, in a series of threats that would fall under the
category of *brosis*.

But just as easily, this could be decay or rot, and in fact, the
English Standard Version has gone with "rust" in their translation.[65]
I think that's better, because it seems to me that Jesus is speaking
more comprehensively here. The threat isn't just rats or vermin;
it's not even just rust. It's the fact that consumption happens. It's
the fact that things decay, that things break down, that things fall
apart, and that things get consumed. The idea is that any time
you put too much trust in something vulnerable to consumption,
it's always going to be precarious. In fact, I think he's building an

argument here, because he talks about things vulnerable to moths and mother nature; he talks about treasure in jeopardy of rust and decay; he talks about wealth at risk to thieves and bad intentions. Each of these examples compounds the idea that happiness built on consumption is inherently insecure.

Martin Luther noticed this and wrote that the great idol mammon has appointed three trustees to remind us of the temporality of our possessions.[66] That word *mammon* comes from the last part of what we read here: Jesus says, "You cannot serve both God and money" (Matthew 6:24). However, in the original text, it's the word *mammon*, a word borrowed from Aramaic that can refer to money in a narrow sense, but also to wealth in a more general sense—maybe even the worship of wealth, in the fullest sense of the word.[67] So Luther read this section and realized that the very fact wealth can be consumed, the fact it can be eaten away, the fact it can be stolen from us, should be enough to remind us not to worship it. It's the very vulnerability of wealth that ensures that once we start worshiping it, we have to keep pursuing it, which is incompatible with statements like "Jesus is Lord."

Wealth is great, and it can do a lot of good. It can create access and opportunity, just like the wealthy landowner who represented the kingdom of God—as long as we remember what wealth is for and don't make it a destination unto itself.

HEBREW IDIOMS ARE A DIME A DOZEN

What about this section in the middle? Jesus starts by talking about wealth that can be used up or stolen. He ends by talking about wealth that can be positioned against God when it supplants God. But then, in the middle, he takes a detour into eyes and bodies and lamps and health, and it all seems a little off topic, doesn't it?

Let's go back and take a closer look at verses 22 and 23: "The eye is the lamp of the body. If your eyes are healthy, your whole body will be full of light. But if your eyes are unhealthy, your whole body will be full of darkness. If then the light within you is darkness, how great is that darkness!" Now, if you pull this out of its context, Jesus sounds like he's talking about what you watch. Perhaps you've heard this used to suggest that you shouldn't watch bad movies, or listen to rock and roll, but that would be a very weird topic to address between two sections that are clearly about wealth. And what we're missing here is that we don't speak the language, or more accurately, the languages.

You see, biblical translation is a tricky game. Not only are you translating one language with a different structure and grammar and syntax into another, but in the case of Jesus, you are very likely taking a Greek translation of an Aramaic sermon that is dependent on Hebrew sayings and trying to turn all of that into intelligible English that flows nicely. Here in the Greek, what we have is literally a sincere eye[68] and a wicked eye. But if you're a Greek speaker, it's likely that what you would take from that is the image of healthy eye and a diseased eye, just like the NIV has translated it. The problem is that Jesus was almost certainly not speaking Greek; he was most likely speaking Aramaic when he gave the sermon. And just to complicate things a little more, what he's using here is a Hebraism, or a Hebrew idiom.

Now, the difficulty with idioms is that they are very hard to translate. After all, they don't mean what they literally say. If I were to say "a dime a dozen," you would know what I mean, which isn't anything related to either dimes or dozens. So, when you hear someone talking about translation and wanting a word-for-word literal translation of the Bible, this is a problem. "Word for word" will have you talking about dimes and dozens instead of what Jesus is really getting at, which in this case is wealth.

In Hebrew, an *ayin-tov* is a good eye, and *ayin-ra* is an evil eye. These were idioms for generous or stingy people.[69] Here are some examples: Proverbs 22:9 says, "The generous will themselves be blessed, for they share their food with the poor." Or more literally in the Hebrew, "A good eye is blessed because he gives his food to the poor." *Ayin-tov.* Now flip to Proverbs 23:6 and you'll find, "Do not eat the food of a begrudging host, do not crave his delicacies." Or again, more literally what we read is, "Do not eat food from an evil eye—*ayin-ra*—do not desire his savoury foods."

In other words, Jesus is still talking about wealth and greed and generosity here.

Jesus says, "Don't invest yourself in what can rust or rot or be stolen; instead, invest in something more true, because your eyes are really the key, and your outlook on the world is what is most important. If you are generous, everything in you will be full of light, but if you're stingy and greedy, everything goes dark. So here's the hard truth: you will serve something—but you can't serve two things, so choose wisely, child."

All of a sudden, a sort of a strange passage where Jesus seems to be bouncing around without much discipline really starts to come into focus. Jesus takes this Hebrew idiom that most of his audience would have been entirely familiar with, and he starts to play with it in some really surprising ways. He starts by saying that the eye is the lamp of the body. For a Hebrew audience, this would immediately evoke Psalm 119:105: "Your word is a lamp for my feet, a light on my path." But then he brings in the *tov-ayin, ra-ayin* idioms from Proverbs and says that generosity is what fills you with light while greed leaves you stranded in the dark. That choice—whether you know it or not—is what ends up guiding you through life.

What Jesus seems to be saying here is that a good life finds its climax in generosity, or that the word of God, meant to guide our path in the world, finds its fulfillment when we become truly generous and gracious in the world.

THE GOOD LIFE

What's on offer here is the invitation to follow the generous way of God, and in that, to find ourselves free from the coveting that damages us. Perhaps generosity was always the lamp that was intended to lead us into the good life, and maybe the antidote for our greed and the unhappiness was always learning to let go?

Now, I'm not talking about salvation here; I'm not talking about heaven here. I'm not talking about the grace that welcomes you into the heart of God. I'm talking about the good life that Jesus says only exists on the other side of a good eye. The life that you were meant for, the one that you are chasing right now—the one we often think more wealth will give us.

Because being generous, sharing what you have, opening your story to another, extending yourself beyond yourself, and yes, giving to your church or your community, was never meant to be obligation or duty. It was always supposed to be an investment in the life you were meant for.

Generosity was never about these broken theologies that tell us we will get it all back and more—you won't. It was about the idea that your wealth, your resources, your talents, and your passion and compassion all were always meant to be shared. You are your brother's keeper after all, and this is where your happiness is buried, waiting to be discovered.

So store up all that you have been given by investing it wherever it is most needed. May generosity light your path, and may your life be filled with light because of it. May you pursue the good life with everything you have been gifted, and may divine satisfaction find you as you do. And recall: "Look at the birds of the air; they do not sow or reap or store away in barns, and yet your heavenly Father feeds them. Are you not much more valuable than they? Can any one of you by worrying add a single hour to your life?" (Matthew 6:26–27).

WORKBOOK

Chapter Eight Journal

Journal Prompt: Reflect on the ideas of greed and generosity in this chapter: *If you are generous, everything in you will be full of light, but if you're stingy and greedy, everything goes dark.* How does the way Jesus talks about money, greed, and generosity touch your life? Take a hard look at yourself, your life, and your priorities. Where is your heart?

_____

_____

_____

_____

_____

_____

_____

_____

_____

_____

_____

_____

_____

CHAPTER NINE

JUDGING AS GOD JUDGES

Do not judge, or you too will be judged. For in the same way you judge others, you will be judged, and with the measure you use, it will be measured to you.

—MATTHEW 7:1–2

WE ALL KNOW PEOPLE who seem hypocritical, which can infuriate us—but honestly, how can any of us ever get our motives fully in check? I want to be a good person, I want to be generous, but I am always pulled in the direction of my ego. How can I ever do anything purely enough for God?

Well, that's a good question, but I've often thought that the very fact I struggle with it might be, at least, the start of an answer. We are social creatures by design; we are drawn to community, and we all need love and praise. Human beings fundamentally need to be acknowledged by their peers in order to actualize themselves. So feeling that tension, being drawn both to generosity and acknowledgment, is, I suspect, normal.

I don't think that Jesus is encouraging us to seclude ourselves, or to live our lives in some kind of anonymous bubble. Remember,

Jesus also tells us to gather and pray with each other, and we all know that we have been inspired to generosity by seeing someone else's life. So this isn't about Jesus enacting a new law; this is about what drives us.

I would probably argue that anyone like me, who pursues a career that involves speaking in public regularly, and specifically about the Divine, has some ego issues to wrestle through. How do you spend all week preparing to present yourself in the best light and then turn around and honestly say your intent is pure? For me, that always comes back to asking the question: can I regularly, consistently, honestly ask myself what is it that drives me?

I know my ego is in there, I know it's part of the mix, and I know I won't ever achieve humility in the model of Jesus. But maybe I don't need to, if I can at least find the courage to be honest with myself. I find this when I regularly ask myself the questions: Am I here because I want to help? Am I here because I have something to offer? Am I here because I am leaning into the purpose and the passion God has given me today?

Then I don't need to beat myself up over the fact that I'm human and that there are all kinds of competing intentions within me in any given moment. When I'm honest and I'm aware, I can choose to move toward the best of those intentions. I can lean into the person I'm becoming, and I can trust that as I do, Christ will meet me, and work with me, and transform me for the better. So, if you worry about your intentions, trust the fact that your desire to find your way toward God is pleasing to God, and that realization itself will slowly begin to change everything about you.

But, what happens when we externalize all of that and when we start to judge each other?

ESCAPING JUDGMENT

We continue with Jesus into some of his hardest words for us as we follow him into a conversation about judgment. I say this is hard, because honestly, who doesn't love to judge? What other reason is there to watch reality TV except to sit back, smug and satisfied, comfy on our couches, judging the participants? That's why reality TV was invented. And yet, in Matthew chapter 7, starting in verse 1, Jesus says:

> Do not judge, or you too will be judged. For in the same way you judge others, you will be judged, and with the measure you use, it will be measured to you.
>
> Why do you look at the speck of sawdust in your brother's eye and pay no attention to the plank in your own eye? How can you say to your brother, "Let me take the speck out of your eye," when all the time there is a plank in your own eye? You hypocrite, first take the plank out of your own eye, and then you will see clearly to remove the speck from your brother's eye.
>
> —Matthew 7:1-5

So Jesus starts by saying, "Do not judge, or you too will be judged. For in the same way you judge others, you will be judged, and with the measure you use, it will be measured to you." There are two interesting ideas for me here. First is the idea that we can possibly escape judgment for ourselves by refusing to judge those around us, and second is the idea that if we can't do that, perhaps we can at least shape our judgment in positive ways for ourselves.

"Do not judge, or you too will be judged." The issue here is, I think, that sometimes what we want to do is universalize the particular, meaning that we want to take one line from Jesus, that applies to a specific conversation or moment or situation, and universalize it into a rule that stretches across all of time and space. The word here for *judge* is the word *krínō* in Greek. It's important to realize that this is not necessarily a heavy word like *judgment* tends to be in English; this is just the simple, normal word for making a decision or a choice. It means to prefer or select.[70] It does not imply you are necessarily vicious in your judgments.

In John 7, Jesus says not to judge by mere appearances; judge correctly. Same word. So the idea here is not that we can't or shouldn't or won't ever make judgment calls in life—that's not realistic. The idea here also isn't that we can seek to avoid judgment, either in other people's eyes or in God's eyes. The implication is that a normal, healthy, positive practice of judgment can, very easily, turn into something vindictive and toxic if we let it.

SHAPING JUDGMENT

This brings us to that second question: if we can't escape judgment, can we at least shape it to our advantage? Now, cards on the table here, I am firmly of the belief that God is for us, that God is on our side, and that God will do good for all of us in the end, but that does not mean I believe we will escape the judgment of God. As I see it, judgment by one who loves us, by one who is looking out for our best interest always—who wants the best for us and wants the best in us—is not something to be avoided, anyway. In fact, I would argue that that kind of judgment, when genuinely divine, is something to run toward.

Just listen to how Jesus talks about this. He says, "In the same way you judge, this is how you will be judged, and the measure you use will be measured against you." From the outset of this discussion, the posture of Jesus, even in judgment, is divine generosity. Our position in the universe is always going to mean that our ability to judge rightly will always be filtered through a glass very darkly. But Divine judgment is inherently different because God's perspective is unencumbered by our limitations and biases.

I don't think Jesus is saying that you can go out and rob a bank and then get to heaven and say, "Well, technically, God, I never judged anybody else on their bank-robbing ways." But maybe Jesus is saying that if your judgments are generous and gracious—if your judgments are intended to bring out the best in those around you, just like I believe God's are—and have been intended to heal instead of punish—to build up instead of tear down, to look out for those around you rather than yourself—then your judgments will be better aligned with God's. And maybe exercising judgment of this kind will actually be your entry point into the process of restoration God has always wanted for you.

Strangely, I find Jesus' words about judgment incredible comforting when I consider that God is always for me. Because this leads me to conclude that divine judgment will only ever heal me—to trust that if I have hurt you, if I have wounded you, intentionally or otherwise, I want you to judge me, carefully and graciously and honestly and personally. Because somewhere inside, I know that my injury of you is injury to myself, and the only way I can begin to heal all of that is to become aware of all of this. When judgment is genuinely for our good, even the moments we try to run from can touch us.

OUR HYPOCRISY

And this is why, after telling us not to judge, after telling us to be careful when we judge, Jesus now tells us how to judge. He says, "You hypocrites, first take the plank out of your own eye, then you will see clearly enough to remove the speck from your brother's." And here we start to see that the whole point of this section was to get to honest, helpful, other-centred judgment that helps each of us become the best version of ourselves.

So, now we've got to ask, what does it mean to take the plank out of our own eye? And what does it mean to take the speck from our neighbor's? There are a couple things that are important here. First is the idea of hypocrisy. The word *hypokritēs* is actually the word for an actor in Greek.[71] In ancient Greece, theatre actors didn't just play a part—they would wear a mask that indicated their part.

It's largely in the wake of Jesus that *hypocrite* takes on its modern connotations. At the time, it would have been heard more simply as "actor." I think this is important for us because "hypocrite" feels so negative and confrontational. For Jesus to call us hypocrites feels unnecessarily mean, so we instinctively tend to shift the narrative a bit: he's not talking about us, we think; he's talking about *them*.

Except we know Jesus really is talking about us here. In his audience are rural Jews, religious elites, Roman centurions, and day-laborers from the Decapolis. So this is not an invective pointed at the overly religious; this is for all of us, all the poor in spirit who are blessed because the Divine has come near to us. Instead of reading "you hypocrites," I find it helpful to go back and read, "All you who feel the need to play your part." Because I'm not a hypocrite, at least I don't like to think about myself that way; however, I know I play a part at times. I know I protect my role at times. I know, as we talked about in the beginning of this chapter, I project a preferred version of myself at times, particularly when I'm feeling insecure. And so, reaching back behind the loaded connotations of the word *hypocrite* in English, remembering that in context Jesus is speaking much more casually, helps me to internalize what Jesus is saying—that sometimes my faults are easier to notice in someone else than they are in myself. Once I can do that, there are two other things that I notice.

First, that Jesus is bang on when he uses the words *dokos* and *karphos*; in the NIV, that's *plank* and *speck*. But more literally, it's *log* and *twig*. Part of the brilliance here is that they are basically the same thing. A log is a twig; a twig is a log—it all just depends on your perspective. Because part of the image here is obviously the hyperbole: how could you ever have a log in your eye? But for all intents and purposes, a twig in your eye might as well be a log.

You might resonate with this, but here's what I notice about myself: the first faults I recognize in you are invariably things that frustrate me about myself. You know what really annoys me? What will set me off and send me into a spiral of negative thoughts? Loud, opinionated, long-haired men who think they get to speak for God. Okay, maybe not the long-haired part—I like that part—but for the most part, the things we instinctively notice in others are the things we struggle to keep balanced in ourselves.

As the type of person who tends to want to dominate the room and fill a moment of silence with their opinion or preference, this same tendency in others drives me nuts—perhaps because I instinctively think that's my job! But when I see the worst of myself in someone else, I can project all of that on them and externalize that discomfort. The twig in my eye that sometimes seems so large and imposing up close begins to fade away until all I can see is what's wrong over there.

Now, the corollary of what Jesus is saying here is that what you notice over there is probably the same thing you should be aware of up close. Don't ignore that. Recognize that your instinctive frustration, your primal rage about them, can actually be a gift back to you if you learn to channel it appropriately. So, know this: the difference between a log and a twig is largely perspective. Jesus is not saying you are worse than your brother; Jesus is saying that you might not be seeing things objectively. The key is recognizing this lack of objectivity.

And this is important because you will *never* see things objectively. Sorry. Objectivity is not a thing that can exist for you. Everything in your life is filtered; everything in your life is colored; everything in your life is seen through the lens of your experience and your position and your history. But Jesus' words highlight that once you acknowledge this, you will actually have something incredibly valuable to share with those around you.

SEEING AND HELPING

The word in the text used here for "see clearly" is *dia-blepo*. *Blepo* is the normal word for seeing or sight, while *dia* is the preposition that indicates a marker of extension through an object. That might sound fancy, but basically, in Greek, they use *dia* the way we use *via*. You got to work today via your car, or via the road system. You entered your house via the door. So *blepo* is to see, but *dia-blepo* is to understand via our sight—"to see clearly."[72]

This is really what Jesus has been getting at all along: good judgment involves more than just what you see on the surface. It involves your heart and your spirit, your willingness to look inward, your best intentions, and your hopes for another. Good judgment is much more than just being objective. Good judgment is about that which chooses to be on God's side, which is the side of the best possible outcome for all.

This is why when all is said and done, when we have begun to understand grace, when we have looked inside ourselves, when we have done our own work, and when we have chosen the best, Jesus says, we will finally see clearly enough to help each other through judgment. In the end, for Jesus, we need each other. His teaching here is not designed to say, "Let everyone do their own thing. Let each to their own; no judgment is good judgment." He's actually saying something much more profound and far more compelling—that we need each other. But we need each other to be *for* each other.

That leads us right into the next line from Matthew, where Jesus follows up his statements about planks and eyes by saying, "Do not give dogs what is sacred; do not throw your pearls to pigs. If you do, they may trample them under their feet, and turn and tear you to pieces" (Matthew 7:6). Now, it's sort of a strange statement, and sometimes people wonder what to do with it. But the key is understanding that while Jesus is changing metaphors, he's really sticking with the same idea. In verse 5, he talks about doing our own internal work, but now he talks about our interpersonal work.

This scripture tells me that before we ever take it upon ourselves to initiate a hard conversation with someone else, there are actually two sets of questions we have to ask ourselves. The first is: am I ready? Have I done my work? Have I uncovered my bias? Am I ready to be humble in offering myself to another? But second is: have I earned the place to speak just yet? Is this other person ready to hear me? Have I demonstrated my care and my concern and my love beyond question in their eyes already? Because if not, well, then they may not hear my words as intended.

I know we tend to hear this and think about dogs and pigs, and we assume they're the problem in the story, but consider this: if you try to feed pearls to pigs, and they're annoyed because pearls aren't what they need right now, who is really at fault? What I understand Jesus as saying is that it doesn't matter how right you are, how wise you are, how well-intentioned you are—if you are sticking your opinions, your perspectives, your solutions, even your pearls of wisdom where they are not wanted or needed, you need to learn to take a seat.

Again, we need each other, and at times we even need each other to judge each other. But it's only after you have demonstrated your care—shown that you are undeniably on the side of the person you are speaking to—that your pearls will ever be welcomed as the gift they are. Judgment is a gift when it models love.

And if you ever been taught, or have assumed, that the judgment of God is for anything but your good—if you have ever received, from those who claimed to speak on behalf of God, judgment that was less than healing, less than holy, less than the goodness of God poured out for you, or if you have ever been led to believe that you ought to receive less than God's infinite grace from those who serve God—then I am sorry. Because that means we have misrepresented the teachings of Jesus. We have become consumed with twigs and looked past logs. In the model of Jesus, the only ones who get to judge you are those who are already for you. And trust me today, the God of the universe is on your side.

So sink into God's love and find a community that can embody God's grace to you. Know that those who love you most will help you become everything you were meant to be. But for this to be our story, we must judge each other well, so that this will only—ever—be our gift to each other.

WORKBOOK

Chapter Nine Journal

Journal Prompt: Reflect on the graciousness of God's judgment as discussed in this chapter: *If your judgments are intended to bring out the best in those around you, just like I believe God's are—and have been intended to heal instead of punish—to build up instead of tear down, to look out for those around you rather than yourself—then your judgments will be better aligned with God's.* What do you feel when you think of God's judgment as being gracious and generous? How does that affect the way you see yourself, your life, your past, your mistakes, and your future? How does that affect the way you see and treat those around you?

_____

_____

_____

_____

_____

_____

_____

_____

_____

_____

CHAPTER TEN

ASKING, SEEKING, AND KNOCKING

JESUS IS STARTING TO bring his first sermon to a close, but he still has some really big ideas for us to ponder. In Matthew 7:7–12, Jesus says:

> Ask and it will be given to you; seek and you will find; knock and the door will be opened to you. For everyone who asks receives; the one who seeks finds; and to the one who knocks, the door will be opened.
>
> Which of you, if your son asks for bread, will give him a stone? Or if he asks for a fish, will give him a snake? If you, then, though you are evil, know how to give good gifts to your children, how much more will your Father in heaven give good gifts to those who ask him! So in everything, do to others what you would have them do to you, for this sums up the Law and the Prophets.

It's a bit of a varied discussion here. We're moving from asking, seeking, and knocking, to fish and bread and snakes and stones, and then finding our way all the way back to the law and the prophets. But this opening line, "Ask and it will be given"—this sounds like a pretty straightforward prosperity gospel, "name it and claim it" kind of moment. If you want it, God wants it for you.

And unfortunately, that is exactly how it has been used at times. Now, I'm going to suggest that's probably not the case. In fact, I'm going to suggest that God giving us exactly what we think we want sounds like a terribly unloving idea.

Once I was getting some hockey equipment ready, fixing a screw that had come loose on my helmet. My son, who was five at the time, was watching, and he asked if he could try on my helmet. I said, "Sure." However, when I went to put it on him, he immediately said to me, "Actually on second thought, that helmet is very stinky, and I do not want it near my face." I thought, "Fair, but also, you're never going to be a hockey player with that attitude."

The point being, we frequently ask for things that seem much better on paper than in reality, and any theology that doesn't account for that seems woefully naive at best. So let's take a closer look at what Jesus is actually saying here.

WHO DO WE ASK, SEEK, KNOCK?

First, Jesus starts into this section with very little context and says, "Ask and it will be given to you; seek and you will find; knock and the door will be opened to you" (Matthew 7:7). And this is really interesting because I think we tend to assume that Jesus is obviously talking about asking God, but he doesn't actually say that, at least not yet.

Granted, he is going to give some context later to clarify that he ultimately has God in mind here. But given where the sermon has just been—a deep, introspective look at ourselves, followed by an emphasis on the need to be cognizant and careful in our speech to each other—I think that if you were hearing this as part of a larger sermon, following along with Jesus as he teaches, your first instinct here might actually be to assume he is talking about us.

First take the plank from your own eye; then you will see clearly enough to help your neighbor. Don't throw your pearls where they are not welcome; instead, earn the right to speak your truth. For those who take a posture of asking, listening, knocking, and waiting to be invited in, they will have the door opened to them. Or, in other words, if you want to be a good friend, if you want to be humble, if you want to judge well and offer yourself as a gift to those around you, well then, ask where you can help, seek first to understand those near you, and then knock and wait for the door to be opened to you. Eventually, it will be.

Now, I'm not saying this isn't about God—Jesus is going to make a pivot in the next section to broaden the conversation—but as a sermon, this is really just a masterful moment. Personally, I can't stand when preachers make one point, and then another point, and then another point, as if they were unconnected. What I find is that when I'm listening, every time it's abundantly clear that we have finished one section and we're moving on to something else, that's the cue for my mind to wander.

So, when I teach, I always want my transitions to feel the natural movement from one idea flowing into the next. I think the difference between a lecture and a sermon is the difference between the dissemination of information and the performance of a story that draws us in and moves you along through those same ideas.

For me, rather than hard stops and clean starts, good sermons tend to have slippery transitions that move between ideas as seamlessly as possible. I think Jesus understands this better than any of us. His brilliance was more than ideas; it was the performance of them. "Ask, seek, knock" applies just as meaningfully as a conclusion to what comes before as it does in introducing what follows—and that is brilliant.

That said, Jesus is going to transition here to our relationship with God, but part of what makes it so sticky is that he moves seamlessly from us to God as if one relationship were the natural extension of the other. I don't think that's unintended. I wonder if "ask, seek, knock" is as much about our interpersonal dynamic as it is about our spiritual journey. Maybe that's the point.

THE VULNERABILITY OF ASKING

As much as we might initially hear this scripture and think, *"Okay, this is great, we're going to get whatever we want,"* there's something profound here that only seems to connect once we hear the scripture in the larger context of relationship Jesus has been building. Think about it this way: If you walk into a coffee shop, and you ask for a coffee, there is an assumed transaction in that question. They are going to make you a coffee, you are going to give them the designated value of that drink. There's nothing particularly profound in that interaction. It's part of the financial and social contract we all operate within, so no big deal.

Sometimes I think this too easily dominates the way we think of God. Of course, we know we can't pay God back, or we can't buy God off, but we almost sort of think of God in transactional terms, don't we? "Okay, I did my part, I prayed. I was a good person; I gave some money to this or that. Now I get to ask for what I need." And at some level, this is all true—Jesus tells us openly and plainly that we should feel welcome to come and ask and seek and knock, and I think even if our theology were bonkers, God would still welcome our voice. And yet, if we go back to the example of coffee, and we replace walking into the coffee shop with going to a friend and saying, "I'm out of cash, can you buy me a drink?" it does feel very different, doesn't it? It's no longer just a transaction; it's a relationship now, and there's an implied story to that request. It's not an isolated moment—there's a history that has led up to this moment and made it possible. There's self-disclosure in this moment that makes one vulnerable, and there's a future that will be shaped both by the question and by the response that follows.

Sure, the example of a coffee is pretty low-stakes, but what if you went to friend and had asked for a place to stay for a while, or a shoulder to cry on, or an interest-free loan, or for someone to pick you up because you had too much to drink? What if what you needed were more than you could ever possibly pay back? And what if you knew that—and what if they knew it, too?

You see, when we enter this conversation of asking and seeking and knocking through the imagination of God as our vending machine in the sky—when transaction is our framework—I think we seriously miss the moment. But when we enter the conversation though relationship, and when we track with Jesus through his teaching on interpersonal dynamics and we watch him transition to God through that lens, I think we begin to hear things very differently.

All of a sudden, Jesus' teachings on asking are no longer a blank cheque to cash in whenever we want. Instead, they become an invitation to be vulnerable before the Divine. If we hear ask, seek, and knock and our first thought is, "Amazing, now I can get everything that I want," we have certainly missed the point. But on the other hand, if we read ask, seek, and knock and our first thought is, "I'm not sure I'm ready for all that. I mean, I appreciate the offer, I really do, I'm just not sure I'm ready be that vulnerable yet. I'm not sure I'm prepared to be that exposed, even before God," perhaps we would be closer to what Jesus has in mind.

Asking for help—really asking for help, really seeking, really standing at the door pleading for it to open—is a sacred moment of coming to terms with our essential dependence, and that will always take courage. Wanting is easy, and buying is simple. Borrowing and purchasing are second nature to us, after all, but I'm convinced that asking can be a spiritual act of surrender for those of us who are enamoured with our self-sufficiency. And it's only when we begin to see our requests of God in relationship with our requests of each other that this reality comes home to us.

DOING GOOD RIGHT WHERE WE ARE

Now, in that light, Jesus makes the full transition and says, "Which of you, if your son asks for bread, would give him a stone? Or if he asks for a fish, will give him a snake? And if you then, though you are evil, know how to give good gifts to your children, how much more will your Father in heaven give good gifts to all those who ask! In everything you do, do for others what you would have them do for you, for this sums up the Law and the Prophets."

See how easily Jesus transitions here from us to God and all the way back, almost as if they were never separate issues to begin with? But also notice that Jesus refuses to pull his punches: he says,

"If even you who are evil can give good gifts, how much more so can God"

And I think our first response is to get our backs up a bit. I mean, "Jesus, I'm not evil, calm yourself." However, I don't think we should take offence here, because I don't think the point is how bad we are at all. In fact, it's actually the opposite. Sometimes in religious circles, we have this terrible tendency to focus on the worst in ourselves—and don't get me wrong, we all have work to do, and the more work we do, the more God's Spirit is able to show us just how there much more there is still ahead of us. But the focus here isn't our badness; the focus is how much good we can do in spite of our flaws.

Jesus isn't jumping down our throats. I think he's actually communicating something more like: "It doesn't matter how much work you have ahead of you; you are capable of goodness right now, here in this moment. Your mistake yesterday doesn't stop you from being generous today. Your momentary misfire this morning does not mean you can't speak grace and acceptance to those near you right now. In fact, none of your mistakes, no matter how evil you have been, stop you from being better, right here and right now." And there's something incredibly freeing in that realization. After all, if your child asked for bread, you wouldn't give them a stone.

THE DIFFERENCE BETWEEN
BREAD AND STONE

Part of Jesus' point is obviously the absurdity of the images he juxtaposes, but there is another level here as well: In the ancient world, bread was baked in stone ovens. It wasn't formed into trays to create the familiar loaf shape we all know today. It was largely just lumps of dough baked on stone into blobs of bread.

Now, remember, Jesus is teaching in the area of Galilee, right along the ancient shore, where for thousands of years, water has run up on the rocks. This is not the Rocky Mountains, where I live; this is the land of smooth, worn volcanic rock. The comparison is hyperbolic, because no one gives a hungry person a stone, and yet the images seem to be chosen purposefully. Ancient bread looks a lot like a stone. (No comment on its texture.)

Okay, fine, you say, but snake and fish? You're not exactly going to mistake those, are you? Well, the Sea of Galilee was home to a lot of stock that wasn't exactly high-end. Tilapia was the predominant food source, but carp, catfish, and eel were the other majority catches.[73] Interestingly, Jewish people typically didn't eat those, particularly because eel don't have scales, which made eating them against the Levitical dietary restrictions (Leviticus 11:9–12). But they certainly would have caught eels and definitely would have sold them to Gentiles.

The images Jesus chooses here seem far too familiar to be purely coincidental. They seem specifically chosen to illustrate the possibility for deception, and maybe that's part of his point—that asking and seeking and knocking are inherently relational because more than involving what we want, they involve whomever we trust with our ask. Sometimes, the difference between what we ask for and what we need, what we think we want and what we actually desire, is much harder to parse than we imagine. Sometimes, if we're not paying attention, we may ask for one thing and receive another but not even know the difference until it's too late. Maybe what Jesus is implying is that part of our asking is actually about our trusting that the one we ask has our best intentions in mind, regardless of how insufficiently we phrase our request.

I think Jesus is saying that just as we need to be careful about where we offer our help, maybe we need to be cautious about where we ask for help. Perhaps the freedom to come to God in our asking, in our seeking, in our lostness, and in our knocking was never about our ability to get what we want. It was always about trusting God's goodness, which invites us to come and receive and be transformed into an answer for someone else's need.

I know there have been moments in your life that have let you down. You asked, you sought, you knocked, and no one answered. I don't for a second want to minimize that pain, because I don't know why things happened the way that they did. I don't understand where God was in your hurt. But I do know that Jesus tells us over and over again that God is for us and that the way that we connect ourselves with that truth is to be there for each other in this moment, right now.

What Jesus seems to be saying is that the more we come to believe God is for us, the more we will be there to open the door to those who find themselves left on the outside, and this is the brilliance and the beauty of what Jesus offers to us in this section. It's not that God is a vending machine in the sky, the answer to all your problems; it's the conviction that when we believe the God of the universe is actually listening to us, we will instinctively become the answer for those who are still seeking.

May you find in yourself the courage to be vulnerable in your questions and requests, both with God and with those who have earned your trust. And as doors are opened to you, may that become, within you, the courage to open the door for the person who continues to stand outside. Trust that God is good, and in everything, do for others what you would have them do for you, for this sums up the goodness of God and makes real the freedom to come: to ask, to seek, and to knock whenever we need to.

WORKBOOK

Chapter Ten Journal

Journal Prompt: Reflect on the purpose of seeking, asking, and knocking described in this chapter: *The freedom to come to God in our asking, in our seeking, in our lostness, and in our knocking was never about our ability to get what we want. It was always about trusting God's goodness, which invites us to come and receive and be transformed into an answer for someone else's need.* Do you trust God? *Really* trust him? How does that trust impact your desire to become an answer to someone else's need?

_____

_____

_____

_____

_____

_____

_____

_____

_____

_____

_____

_____

_____

CHAPTER ELEVEN

The Hidden Path

WE ARE ABOUT TO get to Jesus' big ending here, but to do that well, and make sense of it properly, we need to quickly gather up where we've been so far.

At the start of Matthew 5, Jesus stands before a crowd drawn from Galilee, the Decapolis, Jerusalem, Judea, and the region across the Jordan—in other words, a motley crew of rural Jews, religious elites and foreign oppressors, and Greek and Roman day-laborers. And he begins, "Blessed are the poor in spirit for theirs is the kingdom heaven" (Matthew 5:3).

We touched on the various Beatitudes in the first chapter of this book, but the key here is understanding that none of this represents anything to live up to. The Beatitudes are Jesus declaring the goodness of God to us, promising that the goodness of God has come near to us. Jesus says you are blessed as you are, because God has come to find you. If we don't get this from the get-go, then everything that follows will be slightly out of focus for us.

Everything Jesus wants to say here, everything in this sermon, is predicated on this good news: God is with you, God is for you, and God is cheering you on and wants your best, because God is always on your side. And the blessings that begin this sermon are not the throwaway, win-over-the-audience filler material. This is the core content of Jesus' message. Everything else is exposition.

From there Jesus says that you are the salt of the ground beneath you and the light of the cosmos above you. You are literally connected to both dirt and stardust. You are loved and welcomed, and you are meant to change the world for the better. However, to do that, you will need to understand the story you are a part of, and for Jesus that means coming to understand the law so well that the rules and guidelines and religious protocol that surround you can become what serves you, not the other way around.

For Jesus, rules that shape you and guide you and keep you safe are good, but when rules begin to constrict and suffocate and steal the life from you—when rules stop you from being kind and loving and Jesus-like—then they have come to master you. And so, Jesus says, "I have come not to abolish the law, but to fill it up, to move it from words on a page that master you to a way of being in the world that you can begin to master."

To do that, he begins by teaching us how to pray—how to align ourselves and our imagination with God's. He reminds us not to let worry steal our moments from us, but to trust and believe that God really does have our best interest at heart. He teaches us how to judge each other well, not to ignore each other but to help with each other's best interest always in mind. He links our connection to God back to our neighbor. He turns even our asking into a posture of open-handed welcome for those left on the outside.

And then he says:

> *Enter through the narrow gate. For wide is the gate and broad the road that leads to destruction, and many enter through it. But small is the gate and narrow the road that leads to life, and only a few find it.*
>
> *Watch out for false prophets. They come to you in sheep's clothing, but inwardly they are as ferocious wolves. By their fruit you will recognize them. Do people pick grapes from thorn bushes, or figs from thistles? Likewise, every good tree bears good fruit, but a bad tree bears bad fruit . . . .*

Not everyone who says to me, "Lord, Lord," will enter
the kingdom of heaven, but only those who do the will of
my Father who is in heaven . . . .

Therefore everyone who hears these words of mine
and puts them into practice is like a wise man who built
his house on the rock. The rain came down, the streams
rose, and the winds blew and beat against that house; yet
it did not fall, because it had its foundation on the rock.
But everyone who hears these words of mine and does not
put them into practice is like a foolish man who built his
house on sand. The rain came down, the streams rose, and
the winds blew and beat against that house, and it fell with
a great crash.
—**Matthew 7:13–17, 21, 24–27**

And then the Gospel writer adds, "When Jesus had finished saying these things, the crowds were amazed at his teaching, because he taught as one who had authority, and not as their teachers of the law" (Matthew 7:28–29). Clearly, there is shift in tone here as Jesus brings this all to a climax.

APPARENT VS. ACTUAL

Let's start at the very end of the passage. The writer of Matthew says that the crowds were amazed at his teaching, for he taught as one with authority (*exousía*)—not as the teachers of the law (*grammateús*). Now, the reason I want to talk about this is because these two words *exousia* and *grammateús* are an interesting pairing. *Grammateús,* the single word translated "teachers of the law," means, "an expert in matters relating to divine revelation, a. specialists in the law of Moses: *experts in the law, scholars versed in the law . . . .*"[74] Sometimes it will be rendered "scribes," but what it refers to is the religious authorities.

Exousía means, "the right to control or command, *authority, absolute power, warrant,*"[75] but it seems to me that the writer has chosen these two words on purpose, because the contrast is central to the Sermon on the Mount itself. That real authority comes not from titles, positions, power, and privilege, but from the content of our lives as we share them with each other.

On a recent election day in Canada, when I picked up my son from school, he said to me, "Dad, did you know there was an election today? And do you know how people voted?"

I said not yet, and he said, "Well, do you know who I hope people voted for? I hope people voted for whoever Mom voted for, because she's the wisest in our family." And then he paused and said, "Except on Fridays, then it's you." And then he paused again and said, "Actually, it's me . . . "

Now this is an ongoing joke in our house: that Mom is always right, except on Fridays, which is my time to shine. But as amusing as that is, there's something really profound here—that the authority for my son is not the one who can make the best argument, the one with the most to offer, or the one who appeals to his inherent bias. The authority for my son is the one who has most clearly demonstrated her wisdom and commitment to him already.

There is a difference between apparent and actual authority. Apparent authority is the person with the title or the position. My apparent authority at work is the fact that I have a job as the lead pastor of a church. But in community, that really doesn't count for much. What matters is actual authority, and actual authority is the kind that is hard-won. It's earned through commitment; it's demonstrated through trustworthiness. It's the kind that never assumes anyone ever has to buy in, but gets up every morning ready to earn it all over again.

I am fascinated by the fact that the Divine would choose the path of greatest resistance when it comes to establishing God's authority in the world. When God wanted to speak to us, God chose the voice of one without apparent authority, without credentials, without privilege, and without the assumptions of clout that come with certain markers we cling to.

There are theologies that in the end seem to come down to: God is bigger than you, God is more powerful than you, and God will do terrible things to you unless you submit. Therefore, you should worship God because God demands it. To me, that seems

inherently opposed to the God who would come to us in Jesus—
who was, in an earthly sense, devoid of privilege and absent of
power. A demanding God doesn't seem to line up with a Jesus who
demonstrates the extent of his divine authority through love for us
in his words and actions, to the point of the cross. God's authority
rests on a far stronger foundation than coercion. Rather, it rests on
what God does, which is an extension of who God is—the divine
nature. In this sense, you might say that God desires to earn our
love and respect, as opposed to simply demanding it.

If this sounds strange to you, then perhaps you could think
again about the lengths to which the Gospels tell us God has gone
for you. Authority based on fear can compel you to do all man-
ner of things, but it will never be generative in the way that Jesus
imagines. And when Jesus' words establish their authority in your
heart, I promise you, fear will not be the motivation that moves
you. This is the difference between the *exousia* of Jesus, which you
feel in your bones, and the insecurity of religious leaders who demand you pay attention to them. One is worth your time; the other
is not.

HIDDEN WAYS

However, if that's the case, then what do we do with Jesus' words to
us, "Enter through the narrow gate. For wide is the gate and broad
is the road that leads to destruction, and many enter through it.
But small is the gate and narrow the road that leads to life, and only
a few find it" (Matthew 7:13–14)?

In this last section, Jesus gives us three roughly similar ideas,
built on three different images: a narrow gate, a tree with good
fruit, and a house built on solid ground. Let's take them in turn,
because this is essentially Jesus' argument that we take seriously
everything he has taught us so far.

Sometimes we hear language like this—"broad is the road
that leads to destruction, and many enter through it"—and all of
a sudden, we start to think that Jesus has finally turned on us. But
that's not really what's going on here. Jesus is always for us, always

on our side. Remember, Jesus starts with the declaration that we are blessed exactly as we are, because God has come to save us.

Yet Jesus also recognizes that if we refuse God's coming to us—if we ignore that blessing and continue on the road we have already been on, shaped by religious rules and hard lines, by insiders and outsiders—we will find ourselves inevitably at a dead end.

And this is my frustration with the use of words like *destruction* for *apōleia*. In Greek, this refers to destruction, rubble or ruin, or spoilage or waste.[76] The problem for me is that *destruction* in English seems to imply a destroyer. Now, it doesn't have to, which is why it's not a wrong translation. I just don't think it's a very good one, because it's very clear here that the destruction Jesus speaks of is not something God does to us; it's what's at the end of the road we choose. Or maybe better yet, it's what's at the end of the road we *don't* choose.

And this is really interesting for me, because if we back up and take this entire sermon at a meta-narrative level, Jesus seems to be telling a story that goes something like this: "You are blessed because God has come near to you, offering you a new way to move through the world, and that new way looks like me. And I will gladly let you in on everything I know, because all who seek will eventually find, but the truth is over here, on this way with me. Unfortunately, this way is very easy to miss, and many don't even bother to look for it, which is the real shame."

You see, rather than punishment or retribution, the thrust of this "narrow road vs. wide road" image seems to be the offer of an alternative to the default way through the world. In other words, Jesus isn't threatening destruction; he's offering you a better path than the one you already have.

How many times have you gone on a vacation road trip, and lost yourself to cruise control, following along with all the cars in all the lanes, all driving at the same speed and in the same direction, and been lulled into missing your exit? That, to me, seems more like what Jesus is talking about here—the wide, comfortable road that will gladly take you where you don't want to go if you're not paying attention. This is Jesus saying, once again, that he is for you, that God is for you, and no matter what you choose, that will never change. But everything God offers you exists on the other side of you realizing that the path you're on isn't serving you well.

Reflect back on all the things Jesus has already talked about in this sermon—all of the counterintuitive positions he has offered us. More stuff won't make you any less anxious; more admiration won't make you any more satisfied; more rule-following won't make you more righteous; more opinions won't make you more respected. All the things you've always been taught to believe about how the world works are far less reliable than you think.

And the exit ramp from that way of living is always there. In fact, if you're looking for it, you will find it. But the power of the off-ramp is that you have to want to choose it. In this scenario, life and ruin are not the things God does to us; they are the choice Jesus places before us.

There is a life that lives and breathes and moves through the world with grace and peace—a life that aligns itself with divine purpose. There is a life that embraces our inherent dependence on God and each other, that breathes in full lungs, ready to come alive to every moment. But there is also a life that slinks back into the greed, despair, selfishness, and worry that come so easily to us. Such a life chooses to find its home with all that will one day pass away and be forgotten, like so much rubble.

God will love you regardless of what you choose, but one life is like highway that's easy to stay on and hard to enjoy, while the other is like an off-ramp that you have to be paying attention to notice, but which leads you directly to the trailhead you've been searching for. Jesus is saying, "Please, for the love of God, get off the highway." And that's great, but what happens when we actually choose it?

Here's where we get our second image: a tree with good fruit. And the language here, again, is quite pointed. Jesus introduces this second image by saying, "Watch out for false prophets. They come to you in sheep's clothing, but inwardly they are ferocious wolves. By their fruit you will recognize them" (Matthew 7:15–16a). The idea is, even once you chose a new path, you will still need to decide whom you will pay attention to.

The measure of a person is not their sound bites; it is the fruit of their life. There is a place for writers and celebrities and famous preachers and Bible teachers, but the people whom I allow to really influence me are only the people I have enough access to see up close. Not everyone can be my best friend, and not everyone has the time to mentor me, either, but if I don't have a sense of the fruit in someone's life up close and personal, off the stage and away from the lights, their influence in my life will always be somewhat limited—and I can live with that. There is still lots that I can learn from anyone, but the fruit of someone's life will always overrule the eloquence of their words. Even on the hidden path, choosing whom we listen to is important.

OUR YES AND NO

There is a wide default path in the world that will drag you with it if you're not careful. Then, there is a life-giving side road, hidden in the bushes, just out of view, which is there for anyone to find, but you have to choose it. Yet with any yes come a thousand nos. And this is really what this second image is about for me. Once you get off of the wide road that comes naturally, even once you discover a breath of new life within you, there will always be all kinds of voices encouraging you to get back on the highway.

The good life in Christ can never be about your no. You can never follow Jesus on the basis of what you *don't* do. The idea of following is inherently about moving forward. But every yes does require a no. For example, there are lots of things I am fascinated by and want to learn about, but choosing to be a good theologian means not studying other things as deeply as I'd like. Saying yes to my wife means saying no to other relationships; saying yes to my son and my family means saying no to lots of opportunities to follow my own ambitions.

Again, your life can't be *driven* by your no. That's not healthy; that's not life-giving. That won't provide you with the energy to achieve what you were meant to. But with every yes to which you give yourself, a no will be required somewhere on the other side. When you say yes to the way of Jesus, there will always remain voices in your life that want to drag back into the pursuit of ruin, and you will have to say no. That's okay, because there are voices and choices that do not deserve to come with you as you grow. And the sooner you can make peace with that, the sooner you can get on with the path that lies ahead you.

As Dorothee Soelle writes "The message of Jesus is that the more you grow in love, the more vulnerable you make yourself. You have fewer securities and weapons."[77] Choose what to carry forward. Let go of what holds you back. Trust that Jesus has you.

WORKBOOK

Chapter Eleven Journal

Journal Prompt: Reflect on the explanation of the imagery of the wide and narrow road in this chapter: *You see, rather than punishment or retribution, the thrust of this "narrow road vs. wide road" image seems to be the offer of an alternative to the default way through the world. In other words, Jesus isn't threatening destruction; he's offering you a better path than the one you already have.* How does this description compare to the traditional explanations of this passage, or your own understanding of it? In light of this description, take a look at your own faith and walk with Jesus. What comes up for you?

_____

_____

_____

_____

_____

_____

_____

_____

_____

_____

_____

_____

CONCLUSION

THE POWER OF RESILIENCY

Now we come to the final image in this passage:

> *Therefore everyone who hears these words of mine and puts them into practice is like a wise man who built his house on the rock. The rain came down, the streams rose, and the winds blew and beat against that house; yet it did not fall, because it had its foundation on the rock.*
> —*Matthew 7:24–25*

This is the image we need to hold on to as we leave this Sermon on the Mount. Jesus has welcomed us into the story of God; he has taught about the life we were meant for. Jesus has opened our eyes to glimpse the path on the side of the road, that glinting of a gate we might otherwise have missed.

But the choice to build a life on these words will always still be ours. Whether we embrace that, ignore it, stutter-step over it, or false-start with it, Jesus will always still be for us, God will always welcome us, and we will always be blessed, because that invitation remains forever extended to us.

What Jesus is ultimately talking about here, in the final image of his sermon, is resiliency. When we choose the hidden path, there is a yes and there are a thousand no's, and then there is the continued decision to move in that healthy direction regardless of what life throws at us. The hard beauty of this final image is that regardless of where you choose to build your life, the storm still comes, the winds still rise, the water still flows, and life still happens around you. Jesus has never believed in the way of escape. He has only ever imagined a way of life that has enough resiliency to continue toward the people we were meant to become.

Despite the wide roads, bad storms, difficult moments, and terrible heartache we call life, for Jesus, alongside all of that and often hidden off to the side, there is still grace and peace and joy and celebration. There remains goodness and generosity, sunlight and sand, and stars and beauty, and people who choose to pick each other up, dust each other off, and carry each other forward regardless, because we slowly come to believe in what God believes about us.

And so, when all is said and done, the image on which Jesus chooses to land his sermon is not a fairytale where good choices lead to an easy life. Instead, it's the image of a life convinced of God's goodness and, therefore, resilient enough to hold onto that goodness whatever may come. And that is a way worth following.

Building your life on the foundation of Jesus' teachings is not about getting it all right, or never making a mistake again. It's about building everything on the foundation of God's extravagant love for you, trusting that no matter where you have run or how long it has been since you noticed God's presence, the Divine is looking for you. God is searching you out to bring you home, because you are blessed precisely in your spiritual poverty. And if that can become the bedrock on which you build your life, then storms and wind and crashing waves may distract you for a season but they will never threaten your home in God.

May you notice the path that is just out of view. May the yes that animates you be supported by whatever no's it needs to thrive. May the life of Jesus take root within you so that resilience becomes your story in the world. And may Jesus' words to you in this Sermon on the Mount become more than advice; may they truly shape your way in everything. From the dirt below to the stardust above—and in everything in between—may you encounter the way of Jesus.

About the Author

Jeremy Duncan is the founding pastor of Commons Church in Calgary, Alberta, Canada, an intellectually honest and spiritually passionate community with Jesus at the centre.

He lives in Calgary with his partner Rachel, their dog, and their two adopted kids. Jeremy holds a Bachelor of Theology and received a Master of Arts in Biblical/Theological Studies writing about non-violence and the work of René Girard.

You can connect with Jeremy on Facebook (facebook.com/realjeremyduncan) or find more about the Commons community at commons.church.

Endnotes

1. David Gushee, [@dpgushee]. (2021, May 30). Twitter. https://twitter.com/dpgushee/status/1399017920131440647

2. Amy-Jill Levine, *Short Stories by Jesus*. (San Francisco: Harper-One, 2014), 1.

3. Levine, *Short Stories by Jesus*, 3.

4. Hans Dieter Betz, *The Sermon on the Mount: A Commentary on the Sermon on the Mount, Including the Sermon on the Plain (Matthew 5:3–7:27 and Luke 6:20–49)*. (Minneapolis: Fortress Press, 1995), 92.

5. Frederick W. Danker, Walter Bauer, William F. Arndt, and F. Wilbur Gingrich, *Greek-English Lexicon of the New Testament and Other Early Christian Literature*. *3rd ed.* (Chicago: University of Chicago Press, 2000), 610.

6. BDAG, *Greek–English Lexicon,* 861.

7. Ludwig Koehler, Walter Baumgartner, and Johann J. Stamm, trans. Mervyn E. J. Richardson ed., *The Hebrew and Aramaic Lexicon of the Old Testament*. (Leiden: Brill, 2001), 855.

8. 'the future world,' is . . . the final aeon beyond the days of the Messiah." J. Schneider, Gerhard Kittel ed., trans. Geoffrey W. Bromiley, *Theological Dictionary of the New Testament,* (Grand Rapids: Eerdmans, 1964), v.2:955.

9. Donald A. Hagner, *Matthew 1–13*. Vol. 33A of *Word Biblical Commentary*. (Grand Rapids: Zondervan, 2000), 91.

10. Dallas Willard, *The Divine Conspiracy: Rediscovering Our Hidden Life in God*. (San Francisco: HarperOne, 2009), 114–115.

11. BDAG, *Greek–English Lexicon*, 745.
12. BDAG, *Greek–English Lexicon*, 847.
13. Willard, *The Divine Conspiracy*, 115.
14. BDAG, *Greek–English Lexicon*, 247.
15. Koehler, *HALOT*, 1003.
16. The Holy Bible: *New Revised Standard Version*. (New York: Oxford University, 1996).
17. Jacob Milgrom, *Numbers*, The JPS Torah Commentary. (Philadelphia: Jewish Publication Society, 1990), 154.
18. John Nolland, *The New International Greek Testament Commentary: The Gospel of Matthew*. (Grand Rapids: Eerdmans, 2005), 346.
19. Roy Gane, *The NIV Application Commentary: Leviticus, Numbers*. (Grand Rapids: Zondervan, 2004), 81.
20. BDAG, *Greek–English Lexicon*, 196.
21. BDAG, *Greek–English Lexicon*, 561.
22. BDAG, *Greek–English Lexicon*, 562.
23. Martin S. Jaffee, Stanley D. Golub, *Torah in the Mouth: Writing and Oral Tradition in Palestinian Judaism* 200 BCE-400 CE. (Oxford: Oxford University Press, 2001). 5.
24. Mendy Hecht, "The 613 Commandments (Mitzvot)." Chabad-Lubavitch Media Center. https://www.chabad.org/library/article_cdo/aid/756399/jewish/The-613-Commandments-Mitzvot.htm.
25. Jacob ben Asher, *Tur Yoreh De'ah*. (Israel: Makor, 1987), 371.
26. "*Save life*, 'Pikuach nefesh' ('saving a life') always overrides other Sabbath laws, see 6.5n.; 1 Macc 2.40–41; b. Yoma 84b." Amy-Jill Levine, and Marc Zvi Brettler, eds. *The Jewish Annotated New Testament*. (Oxford: Oxford University Press, 2012) para. 2020.
27. *The Babylonian Talmud*. HolyBooks.com. https://holybooks-lichtenbergpress.netdna-ssl.com/wp-content/uploads/Babylonian-Talmud.pdf.
28. Basser and Cohen give three sources: y. Sanh. 2:6, Exod. Rab. 6.1, and Lev. Rab. 19:2. Herbert Basser, and Marsha B. Cohen,

The Gospel of Matthew and Judaic Traditions. A Relevance-based Commentary. (Leiden: Brill, 2015), 135.

29. BDAG, *Greek–English Lexicon*, 372.

30. "The "liberal" position of Hillel which allowed a man to divorce his wife for such a trivial offense as spoiling a meal." R. T. France, *The Gospel of Matthew*, New International Commentary on the New Testament. (Grand Rapids: Eerdmans, 2007), 207.

31. N.T. Wright, "How Can the Bible Be Authoritative?" NT Wright Page. https://ntwrightpage.com/2016/07/12/how-can-the-bible-be-authoritative/.

32. Betz, *The Sermon on the Mount*, 276.

33. Jacob Milgrom, *Leviticus 23–27. The Anchor Yale Bible Commentary Series*. (New Haven: Yale University Press, 1974), 2138.

34. Rob Reiner, dir. *The Princess Bride*. 1987. 20th Century Fox.

35. David B. Levy, "The Theology, Halakhah, Politics, and Esotericism of the DSS Essene Sect Compared with Normative Rabbinic Practices and That of the Second Temple Sadducees." *Proceedings of the 43rd Annual Convention of the Association of Jewish Libraries*, Cleveland, OH, June 22–25, 2008. https://jewishlibraries.org/wp-content/uploads/2021/03/levy08.pdf.

36. BDAG, *Greek–English Lexicon*, 1085.

37. BDAG, *Greek–English Lexicon*, 475.

38. Walter Wink, *The Powers That Be*. (New York: Doubleday, 1999), 106.

39. Walter Wink, *Engaging the Powers*. 25th anniversary edition. (Minneapolis: Fortress Press, 1992), 185.

40. Brand, Russell. "Vulnerability & Power | Brené Brown & Russell Brand." YouTube video. June 23, 2019. https://www.youtube.com/watch?v=SM1ckkGwqZI.

41. BDAG, *Greek–English Lexicon*, 653.

42. BDAG, *Greek–English Lexicon*, 109.

43. John Sullivan, *Holiness Befits Your House—Canonization of Edith Stein: A Documentation*. (Washington: ICS Publications, 1999), 15.

44. The quotation is widely attributed to Meister Eckhart although the attribution is disputed.

45. Nicholas Wolterstorff, *Justice: Rights and Wrongs*. (Princeton: Princeton University Press, 2010), 110.

46. BDAG, *Greek–English Lexicon*, 247.

47. Betz, *The Sermon on the Mount*, 414.

48. Douglas Sean O'Donnell. *Matthew: All Authority in Heaven and on Earth*. (Wheaton: Crossway, 2013), 172.

49. John Bowden, and Joachim Jeremias, *New Testament Theology: The Proclamation of Jesus*. (New York: Scribner, 1971), 67.

50. BDAG, *Greek–English Lexicon*, p. 737.

51. Moises Silva, Revising Editor. *New International Dictionary of New Testament Theology and Exegesis*, (Grand Rapids: Zondervan, 2014), v.3:567.

52. BDAG, *Greek–English Lexicon*, 197.

53. Howard N. Wallace, *Anchor Yale Bible Dictionary*. Ed. David Noel Freedman. (New York: Doubleday, 1992), s.v. "ADAM(PERSON)," v.1:62.

54. "In the story the woman is called *hawwâ* because she is the "mother of all living *(hay)*." This suggests a derivation from the root *hyh*, "to live." Wallace, *Anchor Yale Bible Dictionary*, s.v. "EVE(PERSON)," v.2:676.

55. "A simpler origin for the name can be found in the Hebrew root *hbl*, those meaning, "breath," Richard S. Hess, *Anchor Yale Bible Dictionary*, s.v. "ABEL(PERSON)," v.1:10.

56. "literary assonance, or a pun, "Cain" *(qayin)* is "acquired" Desmond Alexander, David W. Baker, Eds. *Dictionary of the Old Testament*. (Downers Grove: InterVarsity Press, 2003), s.v. "CAIN," 107.

57. Ron Rolheiser, "A Lord's Prayer for Justice." https://ronrolheiser.com/a-lords-prayer-for-justice/#.XwZDhS2z3OQ.

58. BDAG, *Greek–English Lexicon*, 376.

59. BDAG, *Greek–English Lexicon*, 376.

60. LifeSiteNews. "PopeFrancisWantsChangestoOurFatherPrayer." YouTube video. December 24, 2018. https://www.youtube.com/watch?v=N2vP78LJ4dw. Cf. BBC News. "Lord's Prayer:

Pope Francis Calls for Change." 2017. https://www.bbc.com/news/world-europe-42279427.

61. *Catechism of the Catholic Church* 4.2.3.6. Libreria Editrice Vaticana. https://www.vatican.va/archive/ENG0015/__PAC.HTM.

62. Barry Schwartz, *The Paradox of Choice: Why More Is Less.* (San Francisco: HarperCollins, 2009).

63. K. Weiss, *TDNT*, v.9:70–71.

64. BDAG, *Greek–English Lexicon*, 185.

65. The Holy Bible: *English Standard Version.* (Wheaton: Crossway, 2011). Matthew 6:19.

66. Martin Luther, *Commentary on the Sermon on the Mount.* (Philadelphia: Lutheran Publication Society, 1892), 290.

67. Silva, *New International Dictionary,* v.3:217–219.

68. BDAG, *Greek–English Lexicon*, 104.

69. Bruce K. Waltke, *The Book of Proverbs, Chapters 15–31, New International Commentary on the Old Testament.* (Grand Rapids: Eerdmans, 2005), 237.

70. BDAG, *Greek–English Lexicon*, 567.

71. BDAG, *Greek–English Lexicon,* 1038.

72. Silva, *New International Dictionary,* v.1:521.

73. Edwin Firmage, "Zoology: Animal Profiles: D. Fish." *Anchor Bible Dictionary.* Vol. 6. Ed. David Noel Freedman. (New York: Doubleday, 1992), 1146–1147.

74. BDAG, *Greek–English Lexicon*, 206.

75. BDAG, *Greek–English Lexicon,* 353.

76. BDAG, *Greek–English Lexicon*, 127.

77. Dorothee Soelle, *Thinking about God: An Introduction to Theology.* (Eugene: Wipf & Stock, 2016), 134.

Bibliography

Alexander, Desmond. *Dictionary of the Old Testament*. Edited by David W. Baker. Downers Grove: InterVarsity Press, 2003.

Basser, Herbert, and Marsha B. Cohen. *The Gospel of Matthew and Judaic Traditions: A Relevance-based Commentary*. Leiden: Brill, 2015.

Betz, Hans Dieter. *The Sermon on the Mount: A Commentary on the Sermon on the Mount, Including the Sermon on the Plain (Matthew 5:3–7:27 and Luke 6:20–49)*. Minneapolis: Fortress Press, 1995.

Bowden, John, and Joachim Jeremias. *New Testament Theology: The Proclamation of Jesus*. New York: Scribner, 1971.

Coogan, Michael D., Carol A. Newsom, Pheme Perkins, and Marc Zvi Brettler. *The New Oxford Annotated Bible with Apocrypha: New Revised Standard Version*. Oxford: Oxford University Press, 2018.

Danker, Frederick W., Walter Bauer, William F. Arndt, and F. Wilbur Gingrich. *Greek-English Lexicon of the New Testament and Other Early Christian Literature*. 3rd ed. Chicago: University of Chicago Press, 2000.

Eckhart, Meister. *The Complete Mystical Works of Meister Eckhart*. New York: Crossroad Publishing Company, 2009.

France, R. T. *The Gospel of Matthew, New International Commentary on the New Testament*. Grand Rapids: Eerdmans, 2007.

Freedman, David Noel, ed. *Anchor Yale Bible Dictionary*. New York: Doubleday, 1992.

Gane, Roy. *The NIV Application Commentary: Leviticus, Numbers*. Grand Rapids: Zondervan, 2004.

Gerhard, Kittel, and Bromiley W. Geoffrey. *Theological Dictionary of the New Testament*. Grand Rapids: Eerdmans, 1964.

Hagner, Donald A. *Matthew 1–13*. Vol. 33A of Word Biblical Commentary. Grand Rapids: Zondervan, 2000.

Jaffee, Martin S., and Stanley D. Golub. *Torah in the Mouth: Writing and Oral Tradition in Palestinian Judaism 200 BCE-400 CE*. Oxford: Oxford University Press, 2001.

BIBLIOGRAPHY

Koehler, Ludwig, Walter Baumgartner, and Johann J. Stamm. *The Hebrew and Aramaic Lexicon of the Old Testament*. Edited by trans. Mervyn E. J. Richardson. Leiden: Brill, 2001.

Levine, Amy-Jill. *Short Stories by Jesus*. San Francisco: HarperOne, 2014.

Levine, Amy-Jill, and Marc Zvi Brettler. *The Jewish Annotated New Testament*. Oxford: Oxford University Press, 2021.

Luther, Martin. *Commentary on the Sermon on the Mount*. Philadelphia: Lutheran Publication Society, 1892.

Milgrom, Jacob. *Leviticus 23–27*. The Anchor Yale Bible Commentary Series. New Haven: Yale University Press, 1974.

———. *The JPS Torah Commentary: Numbers*. New York: Jewish Publication Society, 1990.

Nolland, John. *The New International Greek Testament Commentary: The Gospel of Matthew*. Grand Rapids: Eerdmans, 2005.

O'Donnell, Douglas Sean. *Matthew: All Authority in Heaven and on Earth*. Wheaton: Crossway, 2013.

Silva, Moises, ed. *New International Dictionary of New Testament Theology and Exegesis*, vol. 3. Grand Rapids: Zondervan, 2014.

Soelle, Dorothee. *Thinking about God: An Introduction to Theology: Reissue*. Eugene: Wipf & Stock, 2016.

Sullivan, John. *Holiness Befits Your House—Canonization of Edith Stein: A Documentation*. Washington: ICS Publications, 1999.

Waltke, Bruce K. *The Book of Proverbs, Chapters 15–31*. New International Commentary on the Old Testament. Grand Rapids: Eerdmans, 2005.

Willard, Dallas. *The Divine Conspiracy: Rediscovering Our Hidden Life in God*. San Francisco: HarperOne, 2009.

Wink, Walter. *Engaging the Powers*. 25th anniversary edition. Minneapolis: Fortress Press, 1992.

———. *The Powers That Be*. New York: Doubleday, 1999.

Wolterstorff, Nicholas. *Justice: Rights and Wrongs*. Princeton: Princeton University Press, 2010.

CPSIA information can be obtained
at www.ICGtesting.com
Printed in the USA
BVHW041634191221
624259BV00006B/9